I0606144

Epiphany Bakes

BAKERY
WHOLE CLOVES
Today's Picks
• CHOCOLATE MINT BARS
• GINGER COOKIE BARS
• BURNT CARAMEL BARS
• PEPPERMINT

Epiphany Bakes

60 Sweet Recipes from Our Cake Window to Your Kitchen

Melissa Owen

This book is dedicated with love
to my parents, Kamelia & Larry

1 FOREWORD
3 HOW IT ALL BEGAN
15 BEFORE YOU BEGIN

31 Brownies & Bars

52 *This Old House*

57 Cookies

72 *The Cake Window*

75 Simple Cakes & Loaves

112 *Jacinta Sousa*
Friend & Neighbour

115 Fancy Cakes

154 *Ysauld de Montigny*
Epiphany Cakes Production Manager

157 Tarts

172 *Slava Doval*
Dance Fusion

175 Sweets & Sundries

186 *Francyne Laliberté*
Francyne's Cuisine

189 A Few Essential Recipes

220 *Sarah Butler*
Local Author

222 ACKNOWLEDGEMENTS
223 INDEX

FOREWORD

Nestled deep in the BC Interior, Nelson is home to one of the most charming little bakeries this side of the Rockies. As with the town itself, the journey to the bakery is almost as scenic as the destination. Imagine yourself leaving the bustling main street, climbing up or driving past the staircases that pass for sidewalks in this steeply pitched mountain town. You look around, enjoying the 360-degree mountain views and the friendly "hellos" from passing locals, but you're starting to feel a bit . . . hungry. When you reach the leafy neighbourhood aptly known as Uphill, you're greeted by the sweet smell of baking drifting out of an open window. Welcome to Epiphany Cakes!

Here you'll find morning dog-walkers stopping to enjoy a treat in the glorious spring sun, a parade of littles clambering onto the child-size stepping stool to select a house-made ice-cream sandwich on a hot summer afternoon, wool-swathed locals sipping coffee and enjoying slices of cake on a crisp autumn day, and bundled-up adventurers stopping by to fuel up on their way to or from—sometimes to and from—various winter activities.

Epiphany's founder and baker-in-chief, Melissa Owen, has created a beautiful, whimsical delight of a bakery, and the sweet treats within are the expression of a highly skilled and experienced pastry chef and a deeply creative soul. Everything is lovingly crafted from scratch, with an eye for beauty and an attention to detail that makes each item a revelation. The recipes in this cookbook will give you a taste of this experience—familiar for locals, inspiring for future visitors.

One of my absolute favourite items is the iconic Epiphany Lemon Tart (page 165). The pastry is lightly golden, the filling glossy and yellow; the lemon custard is an impeccable balance of tart and sweet and creamy. If chocolate is more to your taste, the Classic Brownies (page 41) and Salted Caramel Tarts (page 159) are guaranteed crowd-pleasers. If your family or guests have dietary restrictions, you'll find recipes, like the Chocolate Quinoa Cake (page 83), that they can enjoy too.

Melissa's passion for her work and the way she and her talented staff genuinely care about their customers shines through the Epiphany Cakes experience, both at the Cake Window and within the pages of this cookbook. Bon appétit!

Sarah Butler
Author of *The Wild Heavens*

How It All Began

Cookbooks are the perfect mélange of my very favourite things:

photography, baking, and writing. The book in your hands is a dream that has been percolating for many years. I love cookbooks and have a ridiculously huge personal collection. I am delighted that my book is now a part of yours.

I took a circuitous route to the life I have today as the owner of Epiphany Cakes in picturesque Nelson, BC.

Food is my love language. I adore preparing it, sharing it, reading about it, photographing it, and of course, eating it. Yet I didn't cook or bake at all when I was growing up. I barely have a single childhood memory that involves me in the kitchen.

I grew up in Bahrain, a tiny island in the Persian Gulf very close to Saudi Arabia. It's so tiny that the letter "B" in "Bahrain" covers the entire country on most maps. My mother, Kamelia, was Egyptian. My father, Larry, was American. The food in our home was always inspired by my mom's heritage. There were no cookies or muffins in our kitchen. I grew up devouring crème caramel, Turkish delight, and baklava.

The flavours of my childhood were a gorgeous, strange hybrid. In Bahrain, it was mangoes, fresh dates, jasmine, phyllo, pistachios, and salty ocean air. In Iowa, where my sister and I spent summers with our grandmother Esther, it was juicy sweet corn, pork and beans, homemade sun tea, and Lucky Charms.

My dad's parents were dairy farmers near the Iowa–Minnesota border. After retiring from farming, they bought a small restaurant called the Corner Café in Lime Springs, Iowa. Growing up, I loved hearing my grandmother's stories about the café, but I never imagined I would one day work in a kitchen myself.

I moved to McMinnville, Oregon, at age eighteen for college. I studied communications and maintained a complete lack of interest in the kitchen. I loved food but had zero curiosity about preparing it. By chance, during my second year at school, I found a job at Piontek's Bakery and Café in downtown McMinnville. The owners, Ken and Peggy Piontek, were a wonderful, quirky pair famous for massive cookies and the best baguettes in the area. They hired me to make coffee and serve customers at the front counter. I enjoyed the bustle of their busy kitchen and the constant flow of delicious baking that emerged from their huge oven. I tasted my first snickerdoodle cookie at Piontek's—something I won't ever forget.

I left McMinnville to begin an MFA program at the University of Oregon in Eugene. I was studying fine art photography, but life continued to gently nudge me into the kitchen. I got a part-time job working at Fenton & Lee, the sweetest little chocolate shop in Eugene's leafy downtown. There, under the watchful eye of the owner, Janelle, I spent my shifts around a large table of women making and packaging chocolates. I loved how Janelle ran her crew and how friendly the work environment was. We rolled truffles, dipped caramels, and wrapped confections in colourful foils while listening to Louis Prima and chatting endlessly.

I enjoyed life in Eugene. I loved being surrounded by art and artists and being creative every day. But after seven years in Oregon, I missed the heat of the desert. It was time for me to return home to the Middle East.

When I was twenty-five, I moved to Dubai and started working at an advertising agency. It felt exciting to be living in such a vibrant, international community. I enjoyed all the luxuries that Dubai had to offer (so much amazing food!), but it was clear that working in an office was not my calling. I did art projects here and there—taking black-and-white photos on the weekends, snapping Polaroids everywhere I went—and became increasingly interested in writing. But I was restless and felt a deep call to spend more time being creative.

In 2000, my mother died suddenly, and I knew that it was time for me to leave Dubai. I ended up in Vancouver, BC, with my new partner, Nick, a scuba diving instructor whom I'd met in Dubai. As I grieved the loss of my mother, I explored our new city. I shopped at the fruit stands, made elaborate sandwiches loaded with cheeses and pesto from the Italian delis on Commercial Drive, wandered around the artist studios on Granville Island, and I began to cook—a lot.

MY FIRST CAKE

One afternoon I decided to try a lemon poppyseed Bundt cake recipe I'd seen in a magazine.

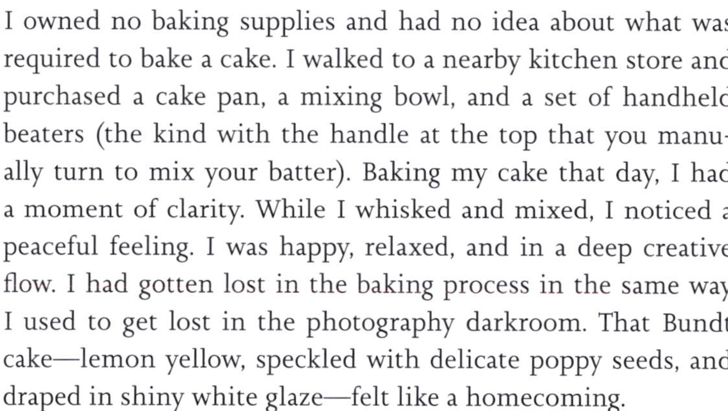

I owned no baking supplies and had no idea about what was required to bake a cake. I walked to a nearby kitchen store and purchased a cake pan, a mixing bowl, and a set of handheld beaters (the kind with the handle at the top that you manually turn to mix your batter). Baking my cake that day, I had a moment of clarity. While I whisked and mixed, I noticed a peaceful feeling. I was happy, relaxed, and in a deep creative flow. I had gotten lost in the baking process in the same way I used to get lost in the photography darkroom. That Bundt cake—lemon yellow, speckled with delicate poppy seeds, and draped in shiny white glaze—felt like a homecoming.

I decided to enrol in the Baking & Pastry Arts program at the Pacific Institute of Culinary Arts on Granville Island. The chefs were French and temperamental, and my days at school were filled with crème brûlée, lemon tarts, and chocolate mousse. We learned how to make baguettes and fougasse. We plated desserts, made caramel, memorized recipes, and hand-rolled croissants. I enjoyed learning about the breads and pastries, but I loved making the cakes. A new world had opened to me, and I was smitten.

One day, while shopping, I spotted a pretty pink card for a business called April Cakes. Eager to learn, I reached out to ask if they needed any help. The owner was a mother of three named April who operated a busy wedding cake business from her duplex off Cambie Street. She invited me to shadow her at work, and we quickly became friends. I baked with her, held her baby, and accompanied her on cake deliveries. A seed was planted. I was inspired by this powerhouse of a woman raising a family and operating a successful business from her home.

After my graduation from pastry school, I got a job working at Meinhard Fine Foods on South Granville Street in Vancouver. I was one of the first to arrive at the store in the dark each morning to fry eggs for breakfast sandwiches, scoop muffins, and make scones and massive amounts of delicious chocolate pudding. Meinhard's was also a great place to spot celebrity shoppers, which I really loved. My next job was at Sweet Obsession in Kitsilano, where I learned how to decorate a huge selection

of fancy cakes, including the most delicious peanut butter mousse cake. (I still dream about it.) From there, I moved on to the Vancouver Art Gallery Café, where I worked alone in the pastry section, baking cakes and making desserts. Baking at the gallery gave me confidence. I was doing it: I was a pastry chef! I worked at the gallery until my son, Nile, was born in 2005, and then it was time to move on again.

NELSON, BC

Shortly after Nile's birth we packed up our East Van home, loaded our new baby, huge cat, and two pugs into a U-Haul, and moved to Nelson, BC. We wanted more space, to own a home and have a yard. Nelson's housing market was more affordable than Vancouver's, and the idea of small-town life really appealed to us. I had never spent much time in the mountains, and Nelson was colder than I was used to, but it captured my heart. In the autumn we bought a run-down house in Uphill, Nelson. To the north of our new home, the west arm of Kootenay Lake sparkled. To the south, the streets petered out into a winding labyrinth of forest trails. Nelson was charming and the people were welcoming. We were home.

Nestled midway between Vancouver and Calgary in the Selkirk Mountains, Nelson is a stunningly gorgeous town. I was instantly attracted to its scenic beauty and glad to discover that folks in Nelson take their food very seriously. For a smallish town (population 11,000), Nelson is a foodie's paradise with an impressive variety of restaurants, bakeries, breweries, distilleries, cafés, and coffee roasters. It has been said that Nelson has more restaurants per capita than Manhattan or San Francisco! It's also home to the Kootenay Co-op—Canada's oldest food co-op.

We delighted in sitting on Nelson's many patios and exploring the cute shops on Baker Street. We were also thrilled to discover farmers' markets, festivals—the Garlic Fest, Jazz Fest, and Market Fest to name a few—and farm stands galore in the area. We bought delicious local produce at the Wednesday Market downtown and at the Saturday Market, which takes place in the shadow of a raging waterfall at Cottonwood Falls Park. (We also discovered that when Nile was fussy in the evenings, we could pop him into the baby carrier, stroll down that waterfall, and the sound of the rushing water would lull him to sleep.)

MY BAKERY

When we arrived in Nelson, I knew that I wanted to open my own bakery.

Nick had started work at Oso Negro, a local landmark café and coffee roaster. While he was away at work, I explored Nelson, and began dreaming up plans for my little bakery.

That spring we replaced the roof on our house and renovated our ground-level basement to accommodate my new business. I decided to call it Epiphany Cakes because of the way that my life as a baker had started with that lemon Bundt cake. The way that baking that cake and making art felt the same in my body had been a life-changing epiphany.

My vision for Epiphany Cakes was to bake everything from scratch using high-quality ingredients. If I wouldn't feed it to my own son, I wouldn't sell it. From day one I baked with organic flour, local eggs, organic sugar, organic carrots, organic lemons, real butter, and real vanilla.

In 2006, I began selling my brownies at Oso Negro. While my commercial kitchen was under construction, I did my baking at the Vienna Café, just off Baker Street. I brought Nile along and he napped in his stroller while I baked. Once my commercial kitchen was complete, I would bring the baby monitor downstairs and bake as much as I could in the hours while Nile was sleeping. My first few years in business, I sold brownies and banana bread to Oso Negro and made wedding cakes during the summer. After that, I added lemon tarts and chocolate quinoa cake to my menu and got a few products into the deli at the Kootenay Co-op.

During the summer season, my friend Sarah Butler and I would set up a table at Market Fest on Baker Street. We had so much fun spending summer evenings selling cookies and cake slices decorated with edible flowers under the warm glow of fairy lights in our market tent (often with our toddlers in tow).

I hired a part-time baking assistant and began to get more custom cake orders. As my business steadily grew, I completed a major renovation to double my workspace and upgrade to professional kitchen equipment.

2023

2006

EIGHTEEN YEARS LATER

It is hard to believe that Epiphany Cakes has been in existence for almost two decades. The bakery still operates from my home on Stanley Street in Uphill Nelson. The kitchen has undergone several more renovations to accommodate a growing staff, a much larger oven, and many more refrigerators. I have a teenage son, an incredible team, and customers who have been with me since day one. Our brownies are still available at Oso Negro, our lemon tarts and quinoa cake are still on the shelf at the Kootenay Co-op, and I have had the privilege of baking thousands of birthday and wedding cakes for the people of this sweet town.

Over the years I have had the opportunity to interact with amazing people and bake cakes for many weddings, birthdays, and special occasions. I have countless stories, like that of my lovely customer Donna, from Fruitvale, BC, who over the course of fifteen years, ordered cakes from me for her daughter's sweet sixteen birthday, high school graduation, and wedding—and most recently ordered a birthday cake for her first grandchild—her daughter's own daughter. It has been such an honour for my cakes to be included in so many of their family's celebrations over the years.

There was a neighbour who asked me to use his own dishes when I made a chocolate mousse cake for his wife's birthday, and to return the dishes to him dirty so that he could put them into their sink and pretend that he had made the cake himself (she didn't fall for it); the lady who asked me to put a carrot cake onto the Greyhound bus to get it to her in Vancouver; and the man who transported a cake to a remote lodge on skis by carrying it in a milk crate on his back (man and cake made it safe and sound). I am delighted to have played a small part in these special occasions and feel incredibly grateful to be a part of my community in this way.

These days, I divide my time between the bakery, the camera, and the computer. I love taking photos of our cakes and maintaining Epiphany's social media accounts. It is not lost on me how fortunate I am to have found my way to this job that I love. I am creative every day, I am deeply content, and miraculously, I still love to bake!

Epiphany products are available all over the East and West Kootenays from Nakusp to Creston. Some of our most popular recipes are included here for you in these pages. What I love most, and what you will find in this book, is simple baking with a focus on delicious texture and rich flavour.

These recipes reflect my story. The Chocolate Halva Cake garnished with pistachios (page 133) is a nod to my Middle Eastern heritage. The Chocolate Mousse Cake (page 139) is reminiscent of the traditional French cakes I made at pastry school. And the Rice Krispie Cake (page 101) is a reminder of my summers spent in Iowa and the classic, simple flavours on my grandmother Esther's table.

This book is a love letter to Nelson, the community that welcomed me almost twenty years ago and has embraced me, my family, and my little bakery wholeheartedly ever since. In addition to my recipes, I am including stories about some remarkable customers, staff members, and neighbours who, each in their own way, contribute to the magic of this very special place.

I hope that you will enjoy using this book as much as I have enjoyed creating it to share with you.

Happy baking!

Before You Begin

A WORD ABOUT INGREDIENTS

At Epiphany I have always used organic flour, local free-range eggs, organic cane sugar, organic carrots, and real vanilla, and I believe you can taste the difference. I have lost track of the number of times that customers have told me that ours is "the best cake they've ever had." While I believe wholeheartedly in our recipes and the skill of my team, I know that the high-quality ingredients we use have a lot to do with the rave reviews as well.

Here's a list of our preferred ingredients at the bakery. These are also the ingredients that were used to test all of the recipes in this book. (Note that this is a list of our preferences, not a list of everything you'll need for every recipe.)

FLOUR

- Organic all-purpose flour
- Organic light buckwheat flour
- Organic brown rice flour
- Organic light spelt flour
- Cup4Cup gluten-free flour

With regular flour, the brand you use doesn't really matter, as they all have a similar composition. With gluten-free flour, however, the brand that you choose can make a huge difference, because not all GF flour blends are the same. Some are mostly rice-based, others are oat-based; some contain xanthan gum, others don't. All the GF recipes in the book were tested with Cup4Cup gluten-free flour. While they should work just fine with other brands, I can't guarantee they will turn out exactly as they do when made with Cup4Cup.

QUINOA

- Organic white quinoa

SUGARS & SWEETENERS

- White sugar: Organic, fair trade cane sugar

The recipes in this book were tested using cane sugar but they will work just fine using any kind of white sugar. Cane sugar is produced from sugarcane, is minimally processed, and can sometimes have a brownish colour from molasses because it's less refined. Granulated sugar (the type most commonly found in the grocery store baking aisle) is produced from sugarcane or sugar beets, is highly refined, and generally very white in colour. Caster sugar, or berry sugar as it's sometimes called, is finely ground granulated sugar. For baking purposes, cane sugar, granulated sugar, and caster sugar can be used when a recipe calls for "sugar."

- Brown sugar: Demerara sugar

Brown sugar should always be packed when you're measuring it by volume.

- Icing sugar (also known as powdered sugar or confectioner's sugar): Finely ground granulated sugar used in cream cheese icing and whipped cream. It should always be measured or weighed and then sifted.
- Molasses: Organic blackstrap molasses

SALT

- Fine grain sea salt

EGGS

- Large, free-range

BUTTER

- Unsalted. I prefer using unsalted butter because it allows you to control the amount of salt that goes into your baked goods.

DAIRY

- Milk: 3.25%
- Whipping cream: 32%–36%
- Buttermilk: 3.25%
- Sour cream: 14%

As you can see, I always use full-fat dairy products.

NON-DAIRY ALTERNATIVES

— Organic unsweetened soy milk
— Unsalted plant-based butter
— Full-fat coconut milk

VANILLA & OTHER EXTRACTS

— Always real vanilla extract, never imitation.

I buy vanilla beans for making vanilla extract (see page 213) at slofoodgroup.com.

— For recipes such as the Lemon Buttercream Cake (page 135) that call for extract, I always use organic, all-natural extracts. I like to buy extracts from omfoods.com. It's a Canadian company that was started in Nelson and offers a great selection.

VEGETABLE OIL

— Use a light, neutral-tasting oil for baking, such as canola oil, sunflower oil, or light olive oil.

COCONUT OIL

— Organic virgin unrefined

SEEDS

— We use organic pumpkin and sunflower seeds in our Backcountry Cookies (page 63).
— Flax seeds: Organic, ground

NUTS

— Unsalted, raw

NUT BUTTERS & TAHINI

— Use all-natural nut butters with no added sweeteners, organic when possible. The same goes for tahini. Natural nut butters and tahini often have a layer of oil on the top. Be sure to stir them well to incorporate that oil before measuring, otherwise your final product may be too oily.

COCOA POWDER

— We use Dutch process cocoa powder in all of our products.

DARK CHOCOLATE & CHOCOLATE CHIPS

— We use Callebaut 54.5% bittersweet chocolate callets for almost everything. Callets (pronounced KAL-ays) are chocolate buttons designed for use in baking and chocolate-making. They are incredibly versatile and higher quality than standard chocolate chips.

Chocolate callets are available in the bulk section of some grocery stores. If you can't find them, you can use a good-quality chocolate bar chopped up into small pieces.

Good-quality chocolate contains some form of cocoa as the main ingredient. The percentage you see on chocolate bars refers to the total percentage of the chocolate that comes from cocoa beans (also known as cocoa mass). The higher the percentage of cocoa solids, the less sugar and other additives the chocolate contains.

You will notice that some recipes in this book call for dark chocolate while others call for chocolate chips. Standard chocolate chips (the kind you find in bags in the baking aisle) are less expensive and are just fine for some recipes (for example, Loaded Cardamom Banana Bread [page 107]); however, they should never be used for any recipe that calls for melting the chocolate (for example, Chocolate Mousse Cake [page 139]). Chocolate chips contain additives to help them hold their shape, making them more difficult to melt. If you are melting chocolate down, always use high-quality chocolate. This applies for dark, milk, and white chocolate.

For vegan recipes, such as Vegan Brownies with Smoked Sea Salt (page 37) and Double Chocolate Ginger Chippers (page 61), be sure to read the ingredients on your chocolate carefully, as some dark chocolate contains dairy.

FRUITS & VEGGIES

— When a recipe calls for fruit, berries, or veggies, we use organic, and local whenever feasible.

We use organic carrots in all our carrot cakes, and organic bananas in our banana bread. I also recommend using organic lemons, especially when you're including lemon zest in a recipe. The surface of conventional lemons contains wax and pesticides, which you don't want to end up in your baked goods.

SPRINKLES

— I love sprinkles. And these days there are so many fun colours and shapes to choose from. I buy sprinkles from sweetapolita.com. It's a Canadian company with a great selection that includes vegan and gluten-free options.

BAKING TOOLS

The items on the first list are basic baking tools, which every home baker should have in their kitchen. The items on the Pots, Pans, Sheets, Etc. list are essential for certain recipes—for example, a 12-cup muffin pan for making cupcakes or a jumbo muffin pan for making Cake-ettes (page 81)—so always read through each recipe completely before you begin to ensure you have the necessary equipment.

The items on the Not Essential—but Really Useful list are more specialized (and sometimes expensive) tools you can consider investing in if you plan to really get serious about baking. A stand mixer, for example, is exceptionally handy, but by no means essential if you're only baking the occasional batch of cookies or brownies.

There is one more list on page 117, at the beginning of the Fancy Cakes chapter, dedicated to the tools required for making layer cakes. Layer cakes require a whole bunch of specialized equipment very specific to the recipes in that particular chapter. If you're interested in making layer cakes, be sure to take a look at the equipment list.

BASIC TOOLS

- A sturdy whisk
- A good-quality silicone spatula
- An offset spatula
- Mixing bowls in a variety of sizes
- Heatproof bowls (stainless steel or glass)
- A rolling pin
- A fine mesh sieve
- A sharp chef's knife
- A paring knife
- A Pyrex liquid measuring cup
- A full set of dry measuring cups
- A full set of measuring spoons
- Parchment paper
- Pan spray

POTS, PANS, SHEETS, ETC.

- Two 8 × 8-inch metal baking pans
- Two 9 × 13-inch metal baking pans
- Two 9 × 5-inch metal loaf pans
- Two 12-cup muffin pans
- One jumbo muffin pan
- Two 13 × 18-inch good-quality cookie sheets
- One heavy-bottomed saucepan
- A set of round cookie cutters

NOT ESSENTIAL—BUT REALLY USEFUL—BAKING TOOLS

Stand mixer

There are many recipes in this book that do not require a stand mixer. But if you plan to get into baking in a serious way, a stand mixer is a great investment. Stand mixers can be used to whip cream, knead dough, and beat butter. In some cases, hand beaters can be used in place of a stand mixer, but certain recipes, such as meringues (page 185) or our Vanilla Buttercream (page 199), should not be attempted without a stand mixer. I have always used Kitchen Aid stand mixers and swear by their reliability. I still use the first Kitchen Aid mixer that I purchased when I was in pastry school over twenty years ago!

Digital kitchen scale

The recipes in this book are listed in both weight and cup measurements. For consistent results, it's generally best to weigh your ingredients. Measuring with cups, while quick and easy, can be inaccurate. Don't mix and match systems, though. If you weigh your flour, weigh your butter, sugar, etc. as well. If you use a cup to measure your flour, do the same to measure your cocoa, sugar, etc.

Candy thermometer

You can certainly get away without one of these, but they're inexpensive—and essential if you want to make caramel or buttercream.

Digital thermometer

A bit more of an investment than a standard candy thermometer but it gives a very accurate temperature reading. Bonus: You can also use it to check if your roast chicken is done.

Wire cooling rack

Allows air to circulate around your baked goods as they cool. Most of my recipes call for removing items from the oven and placing them on a rack to cool. If you don't have a cooling rack you can place your baking pan on an inverted muffin pan to cool your items while they're still in the pan. The goal is to allow for increased air circulation. A cooling rack is also useful when pouring ganache or glaze onto cakes.

Culinary scoop

A culinary scoop is essentially an ice-cream scoop that's used to portion things such as cookie dough and cupcakes. Culinary scoops are available in a variety of sizes and are handy for creating uniform cookies and cupcakes. In addition, using a scoop is much quicker than rolling cookies by hand. At the bakery we use a 2 tablespoon (30 ml) scoop for our Gingersnaps (page 59) and Double Chocolate Ginger Chippers (page 61), and a ¼ cup (60 ml) scoop for portioning cupcakes and muffins.

Microplane

Cake pans

For single-layer tall cakes, such as the Chocolate Quinoa Cake (page 83) and Olive Oil Cake with Rose Syrup (page 91), you'll need an 8-inch round pan that's at least 3 inches tall.

For layer cakes, you'll want to invest in three good-quality cake pans of the same size. My favourite sizes are 6-inch and 8-inch.

For cheesecakes, you'll need a 6-inch springform pan. Springform pans have a removable bottom, making it easy to remove your cake from the pan.

Bundt pan

Bundt pans have a hole in the centre and are available in a lot of pretty designs. Bundt cakes are a nice alternative to a layer cake. They look fancy but are quicker to make. Recipes in this book call for a 9-inch Bundt pan.

Tart tins

Recipes in this book call for using 4¾ × ¾-inch tart tins with a removable bottom. I suggest having 6–12 of them. This size is commonly available online and in kitchen stores. If you can't find the exact size or you already own a different size, don't worry. The tart recipes will work using almost any size tart tin, you might just end up with extra tart dough and filling if you use smaller tart pans.

If you don't have any tart tins or don't want to invest in them, you can use a muffin pan to form mini tarts. Use a cookie cutter to cut 3½-inch rounds of tart dough, press the dough into the muffin cups, and follow the same instructions as for using tart tins. Tarts made this way end up looking a bit more rustic, but taste just as good. Again, you may end up with extra tart dough and fillings if you go this route.

Citrus zester

A great tool for creating thin strips of citrus zest. Bonus: You can also use it to grate garlic and hard cheeses.

Pastry brush

I prefer silicone brushes because they're easy to keep clean. Avoid pastry brushes with nylon or natural bristles, which tend to fall out and end up in your food!

Piping bag & tips

While piping bags are mostly used to decorate cakes, they're also handy for evenly distributing fillings, such as the frangipane in our Strawberry Frangipane Tarts (page 171). I recommend using a medium-size bag (16-inch) with a large round piping tip.

Food processor

Handy for grating carrots and zucchinis.

Blender

We use a high-powered blender to make our Chocolate Quinoa Cake (page 83) batter and blend the flax seeds for our Vegan Brownies with Smoked Sea Salt (page 37). You can also use a food processor fitted with a metal blade.

Crockpot

You'll need a crockpot (aka a slow cooker) to make Apple Butter (page 211). They are widely available, are relatively inexpensive, and can be used to prepare all sorts of meals.

Ice-cream maker

Salted Caramel Ice-cream Sandwiches (page 179) require an ice-cream maker. It's a fun thing to have, but by no means necessary unless you're passionate about ice cream. If you don't have one, don't worry. The Brownie Ice-Cream Sandwiches recipe (page 181) uses store-bought ice cream.

Metal clips

To hold the parchment paper in place on your baking pans. Available at most stationery stores.

TIPS

HOW TO PREPARE YOUR BAKING PANS

There are a lot of elaborate methods for preparing pans for baking, ranging from brushing them with melted butter to prepping them with a "goop" made of flour and oil. At Epiphany we use a combination of pan spray and parchment paper to ensure baked goods don't stick to the pan.

FOR SLAB CAKES, BARS, AND BROWNIES: Spray the pan generously with pan spray and then place a strip of parchment paper down the centre of the pan lengthwise, and another one widthwise. Be sure that the parchment paper is longer than the pan on all sides (this creates handles that make it easier to lift out the cake or brownies after baking). The excess parchment paper can be clipped to the pan with metal clips. While the clips are optional, they help to keep the parchment from folding over into the batter. This is particularly useful if you have a convection oven, as the air tends to blow the parchment paper around—and often into—the batter during baking.

FOR LOAVES AND ROUND CAKES (INCLUDING BUNDT CAKES AND CHEESECAKES): Spray the pan generously with pan spray (no parchment paper required).

FOR COOKIE SHEETS: Line with parchment paper.

HOW TO MEASURE DRY INGREDIENTS USING MEASURING CUPS

When I'm measuring dry ingredients with cups, I use what I call the scoop and scrape method. Scoop the ingredient out of the bag with the measuring cup and use an offset spatula or the back of a knife to scrape the excess back into the bag, leaving a perfectly level cup.

WHICH OVEN RACK TO USE

If you've only got one thing in the oven, always use the middle rack. This places your baked goods an even distance between the top and bottom elements of the oven and allows for even baking.

BE SURE TO ROTATE YOUR PANS

Most ovens have hot spots. Our massive commercial convection oven tends to be hotter in the top right corner, so we always rotate pans halfway through the bake time to ensure even baking. Turn each pan 180 degrees. If you've got things baking on multiple oven racks, switch the pans around onto different shelves as well (pans from the top shelf move down, pans from the bottom shelf move up).

MIXING & MATCHING

I really hope you'll have fun with these recipes.

I also hope that you'll use them as a jumping-off point for your own baking creations.

Don't be afraid to mix and match fillings, cakes, and icings. For example, pair Gingersnaps (page 59) and Aquafaba Vanilla Icing (page 203) to create a vegan sandwich cookie. Jazz up your Banana Bread (page 107) or Zucchini Loaf (page 111) by adding Cream Cheese Icing (page 204). Or make my Tahini Caramel Sandwich Cookies your own by playing with different fillings (such as Ganache [page 205] or Peanut Butter Icing [page 77]).

Consider the recipes in the book's final chapter, A Few Essential Recipes, as a foundation—they can be used in a multitude of ways. The Perfect Vanilla Cake (page 193) and the Epiphany Chocolate Cake (page 191) can be paired with any icing. Our Vanilla Buttercream (page 199) can easily be tweaked by adding extract or melted chocolate. Meringues (page 185) can be added onto any dessert for an element of crunch and whimsy. Tart doughs can be used to create any tart you can imagine, and Salted Caramel (page 210) is delicious drizzled on virtually any cake or dessert plate.

The sky's the limit. Have fun and please tag me when you bake from this book. I can't wait to see what you come up with!

INSTAGRAM: @epiphanycakesnelson

Brownies & Bars

33 Simple Lemon Bars

35 Brownies with Pistachio Cream

37 Vegan Brownies with Smoked Sea Salt

39 Apple Butter Blondies

41 Our Classic Brownies

43 Breakfast Brownies

45 Ube Cheesecake Bars

47 Billionaire's Shortbread

51 Trick or Treat Brownies

52 *This Old House*

Simple Lemon Bars

GLUTEN-FREE
YIELD: 8 bars

INGREDIENTS

BARS

¼ cup (42 g) buckwheat flour
¼ cup (40 g) brown rice flour
¼ cup (25 g) ground almonds
½ tsp salt
½ cup (113 g) unsalted butter, at room temperature
¾ cup (150 g) sugar
Zest of 1 lemon + 3 Tbsp lemon juice
2 eggs
1 tsp vanilla extract

GLAZE

½ cup (65 g) icing sugar
1–2 Tbsp lemon juice

Lemon bar recipes commonly call for a shortcrust layer that is baked, topped with lemon curd, and then baked again. I've never liked that method for making lemon bars. It has far too many steps. I like simple baking that's not too finicky, and I much prefer this style of lemon bar, which comes together quickly and tastes just as good as its more complex counterpart.

METHOD

BARS

Preheat your oven to 350°F. Prepare an 8 × 8-inch baking pan (see page 27).

Sift the flours, ground almonds, and salt into a bowl and set aside.

Place the butter, sugar, and lemon zest into the bowl of a stand mixer. Fit the mixer with the paddle attachment. Beat on medium speed until light and fluffy, about 3 minutes.

Add the eggs to the mixer one at a time. Mix in the lemon juice and vanilla.

Finally, add the dry ingredients and mix on low speed until just combined.

Transfer the batter to the baking pan and bake until the centre is set and the edges are golden, about 20 minutes. Place the pan on a cooling rack to let the bars cool completely.

GLAZE

Sift the icing sugar into a bowl and stir in the lemon juice 1 tablespoon at a time until a smooth, pourable glaze forms.

ASSEMBLY

Spread the glaze over the lemon bars and allow to set in the refrigerator for about 1 hour before removing from the pan and cutting into 8 bars.

Brownies with Pistachio Cream

GLUTEN-FREE
YIELD: 8 brownies

INGREDIENTS

⅔ cup (93 g) gluten-free flour blend
¾ cup (100 g) cocoa powder
1 tsp salt
½ cup (113 g) unsalted butter, at room temperature, cubed
¼ cup (60 ml) vegetable oil
⅔ cup (113 g) dark chocolate callets, divided
1 cup (200 g) sugar
¼ cup (50 g) packed brown sugar
2 eggs, at room temperature
2 tsp vanilla extract
½ cup (150 g) pistachio cream, at room temperature

These may be my favourite brownies ever. And that's saying a lot because I have eaten a lot of brownies. These are fudgy, they come together quickly, and the pistachio cream provides a delicious layer of flavour and texture. Pistachio cream is available at specialty food stores or online. If you prefer, you can use the same volume of peanut butter or hazelnut spread, which are easier to find, but trust me: it's well worth the extra step of tracking down the pistachio cream.

METHOD

Preheat your oven to 350°F. Prepare an 8 × 8-inch baking pan (see pagc 27).

Sift the flour, cocoa powder, and salt into a bowl and set aside.

Place the butter, oil, and half of the chocolate in a heatproof bowl and place over a saucepan of simmering water, making sure the bottom is not touching the water and stirring occasionally, until the chocolate is completely melted. Whisk until smooth and then whisk in both sugars.

Remove the mixture from the heat and set aside to cool for 5–10 minutes. Once the mixture is cool to the touch (it needs to cool down enough not to scramble the eggs) whisk in the eggs and vanilla and then use a silicone spatula to fold in the dry ingredients. Fold in the rest of the chocolate, transfer the batter to the pan, and smooth the top with an offset spatula.

Place dollops of pistachio cream all over the surface of the brownies, and use the tip of a knife to swirl it into the batter and create a pretty pattern.

Bake until the brownies are set and pulling slightly away from the edges of the pan, 20–25 minutes.

Place the pan on a cooling rack. Allow the brownies to cool completely before cutting.

Vegan Brownies with Smoked Sea Salt

VEGAN
YIELD: 12 brownies

INGREDIENTS

¾ cup (105 g) all-purpose flour
½ tsp baking powder
½ tsp salt
1¼ cups (284 g) unsalted plant-based butter, cubed
1 cup + 3 Tbsp (220 g) brown sugar, packed
¾ cup (150 g) sugar
1¼ cups (169 g) cocoa powder
¼ cup (35 g) ground flax seeds
2 tsp vanilla extract
1 cup (170 g) vegan dark chocolate chips
Smoked sea salt, for sprinkling

NOTE: If you can't find unsalted plant-based butter, you can use salted, but omit the final sprinkling of sea salt to prevent your brownies from being too salty.

We bake these deeply chocolatey brownies for our friends at Sprout vegan restaurant. The combination of cocoa powder and dark chocolate in this recipe results in a brownie with an irresistible gooey texture. Sprout, located downtown in Nelson's historic Annable Block, was started in 2018 by Amber Greenleese. Amber and her team pump an impressive amount of delicious vegan fare out of their tiny kitchen. The restaurant is seriously charming, and their patio is an awesome spot to sit and enjoy a tasty meal and watch the world go by.

METHOD

Sift the flour, baking powder, and salt into a bowl and set aside.

Place the butter, both sugars, and cocoa powder in a heatproof bowl and place over a saucepan of simmering water, making sure the bottom is not touching the water. Heat, stirring occasionally, until the mixture is completely melted. Remove from the heat, whisk until smooth, and set aside to cool for about 10 minutes.

Preheat your oven to 350°F. Prepare a 9 × 13-inch baking pan (see page 27).

Combine the flax seeds with ¾ cup (180 ml) water in a blender or food processor and mix until frothy. Transfer the flax mixture to a measuring cup and set aside for 5–10 minutes to thicken.

Once thickened, whisk the flax into the bowl with the butter, sugar, and cocoa powder. Add the vanilla and whisk vigorously until smooth. Fold in the flour mixture and then the chocolate chips.

Transfer the batter to the baking pan and sprinkle with smoked sea salt. Bake until the brownies are set and pulling slightly away from the edges of the pan, 20–25 minutes. Place the pan on a cooling rack. Allow the brownies to cool completely before cutting.

Apple Butter Blondies

YIELD: 16 blondies

INGREDIENTS

¾ cup (90 g) chopped walnuts
1½ cups (210 g) all-purpose flour
1 tsp baking powder
½ tsp salt
½ tsp ground cinnamon
¾ cup (170 g) unsalted butter
1½ cups (300 g) brown sugar, packed
2 eggs
3 tsp vanilla extract
½ cup (180 g) Apple Butter (page 211)

These blondies scream falling leaves and autumnal coziness to me. I love autumn in the Kootenays, when the air turns crisp, apples are in season, smoke starts billowing from chimneys, and we all reach for our woolly socks and cardigans.

METHOD

Preheat your oven to 350°F. Prepare a 9 × 13-inch baking pan (see page 27).

Place the chopped walnuts on a baking sheet and toast in the oven until golden and fragrant, 8–10 minutes. Remove from the oven and place on a cooling rack to cool completely.

Meanwhile, sift the flour, baking powder, salt, and cinnamon into a bowl and set aside.

Melt the butter in a small saucepan over low heat and then transfer it to a mixing bowl. Add the sugar and use a silicone spatula to combine. Add the eggs, one at a time, followed by the vanilla. Finally, use a silicone spatula to fold in the dry ingredients, followed by the toasted walnuts.

Transfer the batter to the prepared baking pan and use an offset spatula to smooth it into an even layer. Place dollops of apple butter all over the surface of the blondies and then use the tip of a knife to swirl the apple butter into the batter.

Bake until the edges are golden, and the blondies are pulling away from the sides of the pan, 20–25 minutes.

Place the pan on a cooling rack. Once the blondies are just cool enough to handle, use the parchment paper to lift them out of the pan. Cut into 16 pieces and serve warm or cold. (I strongly suggest eating them while they're still warm!)

Our Classic Brownies

YIELD: 8 brownies

INGREDIENTS

1 cup (140 g) all-purpose flour
1 tsp baking powder
¼ tsp salt
1½ cups (340 g) unsalted butter
1 cup (200 g) sugar
1 cup (200 g) brown sugar, packed
1 cup (135 g) cocoa powder
3 eggs, at room temperature
1 tsp vanilla extract

These are the brownies that I started my business with back in 2006. I've sold thousands of them over the past 18 years, and I haven't changed the original recipe a single bit. When I opened the bakery, my first customer was Oso Negro, Nelson's legendary café and roastery, famous for their dark roasts. The Oso Negro café is perched on the corner of Ward and Victoria streets in a restored heritage house. It's easy to spot by the line-up, which is out the door most days. On a sunny day their lush garden seating area, always buzzing with house sparrows on the lookout for tasty crumbs, is the perfect place to enjoy a brownie and an Americano.

METHOD

Preheat your oven to 350°F. Prepare an 8 × 8-inch baking pan (see page 27).

Sift the flour, baking powder, and salt into a mixing bowl and set aside.

Combine the butter, both sugars, and the cocoa powder in a medium heatproof bowl and place over a pan of simmering water. Stir occasionally until melted and smooth. Remove from the heat and set aside to cool for 10–15 minutes.

Place the eggs and vanilla in a bowl or measuring cup and whisk to combine. Once the butter/sugar mixture is cool to the touch, add the eggs, whisking vigorously to combine. Use a silicone spatula to fold in the flour mixture.

Transfer the batter to the prepared baking pan and bake until set and slightly pulling away from the edges of the pan, 30–35 minutes.

Place the pan on a cooling rack. Allow the brownies to cool completely before cutting.

Breakfast Brownies

VEGAN, GLUTEN-FREE
YIELD: 8 brownies

INGREDIENTS

2 Tbsp ground flax seeds
⅓ cup (80 ml) water
1 cup (250 g) tahini
½ cup (85 g) coconut sugar
¼ cup (60 ml) pure maple syrup
2 tsp vanilla extract
⅓ cup (45 g) cocoa powder
½ cup (45 g) shredded unsweetened coconut
¼ cup (35 g) hemp hearts
1 Tbsp coconut flour
½ tsp baking soda
½ tsp baking powder
¼ tsp salt
⅓ cup (57 g) vegan dark chocolate chips

This recipe was created by Cindy Spratt, a holistic nutritionist based in Ymir, BC. I got to know Cindy while camping at Fry Creek, a stunning secluded boat-access camping spot on Kootenay Lake. She and I bonded over food (of course) and a love of small dogs. She brought a batch of these delicious brownies camping with her, and I could not get enough of them. They're naturally sweetened, vegan, and gluten-free, but somehow also utterly decadent. They definitely do not taste like a "healthy" brownie. We nibbled on them while lazing on the beach and while hanging around the fire in the evenings—but my absolute favourite time to enjoy them was with my morning coffee, which is why I have called them Breakfast Brownies. As soon as I got home, I emailed Cindy to ask for the recipe. She obliged and has generously allowed me to share it here with you.

METHOD

Preheat your oven to 350°F. Prepare an 8 × 8-inch baking pan (see page 27).

Place the flax seeds in a measuring cup or small bowl and add the water. Stir vigorously and set aside for about 10 minutes to thicken.

Place all the rest of the ingredients into a medium bowl one by one, combining with a silicone spatula as you go. Do not overmix. Fold in the flax seed/water mixture last.

Pour the batter into the baking pan and smooth the top with a spatula. Bake until a knife inserted into the centre comes out almost clean, 25–30 minutes. Be careful not to overbake—you want them to be gooey.

Place the pan on a cooling rack. Allow the brownies to cool completely before cutting.

Ube Cheesecake Bars

YIELD: 12 bars

INGREDIENTS

CRUST

1 cup (100 g) quick oats
⅔ cup (93 g) all-purpose flour
½ cup (100 g) brown sugar, packed
½ tsp baking soda
A pinch of salt
½ cup (113 g) unsalted butter, at room temperature

UBE FILLING

1½ cups (340 g) full-fat cream cheese, at room temperature
4 eggs
2 tsp vanilla extract
1 (300 ml) can ube condensed milk

NOTE: Ube condensed milk is available at Filipino grocery stores and some Asian markets.

I first discovered ube (purple yam) when I visited Lyra Lou Cakes, a bakery in Surrey, BC, that is famous for its ube mousse cake. I was immediately enchanted by its vibrant purple colour and delicious subtle flavour. Soon after, I asked a friend travelling from Vancouver to bring me some ube so I could experiment with it. She showed up with two cans of ube condensed milk (even better!) and these cheesecake bars were born. The flavour of ube is subtle, earthy, and vanilla-like. It reminds me a little bit of taro. It pairs perfectly with the richness of the cream cheese in these bars.

METHOD

CRUST

Preheat your oven to 350°F. Prepare a 9 × 13-inch baking pan (see page 27).

Place the dry ingredients in a large mixing bowl and work in the butter with your hands. Once combined, press the crust into the pan and use the bottom of a glass or your hands to flatten it. Bake until fragrant and lightly golden, 10–12 minutes.

Place the pan on a cooling rack.

Reduce the oven temperature to 250°F.

UBE FILLING

Place the cream cheese in the bowl of a stand mixer fitted with the paddle attachment and beat on high speed until light and smooth, 3–5 minutes. Scrape down the sides of the mixing bowl and the paddle using a silicone spatula as necessary. Add the eggs one at a time, beating well between additions, followed by the vanilla. Remove ½ cup (120 g) of the cheesecake batter from the mixer and set it aside. Add the ube condensed milk to the mixer and mix on low speed until no white streaks remain. Strain the ube cheesecake batter through a fine mesh sieve to remove any lumps and then pour it over the cooled crust.

>>

ASSEMBLY

Use a spoon to place small dollops of the reserved vanilla cheesecake batter all over the surface of the ube batter and then run the tip of a knife through the two batters to mix them and create a pretty pattern.

Bake until firm, about 1 hour. The batter may still have a bit of a jiggle to it, but it should be a firm jiggle as opposed to a liquidy jiggle.

Place the pan on a cooling rack. Once the pan is cool enough to handle, transfer it to the refrigerator for at least 1 hour to cool completely before removing from the pan and cutting into 12 bars.

Billionaire's Shortbread

GLUTEN-FREE
YIELD: 16 squares

INGREDIENTS

SHORTBREAD

1 cup (140g) gluten-free flour blend
1 tsp baking powder
¼ tsp salt
½ cup (113 g) unsalted butter, at room temperature
¼ cup (50 g) sugar

CARAMEL

½ cup (113 g) unsalted butter, cubed
1 (300 ml) can sweetened condensed milk
2 Tbsp light corn syrup
½ cup (100 g) sugar

CHOCOLATE

¾ cup (125 g) dark chocolate callets or good-quality chocolate bar, coarsely chopped
¼ cup (57 g) unsalted butter, cut into small pieces
1 Tbsp light corn syrup
Coarse salt, for sprinkling

NOTE: If gluten isn't an issue, replace the gluten-free flour with the same amount of all-purpose flour.

One of the things I look forward to the most at Christmastime is receiving my annual tin of Billionaire's Shortbread from my friend Tammy Everts. Tammy and I met when we were both living around Commercial Drive in Vancouver and joined a group called Moms with Dogs on the Drive. Our very informal group would push strollers to the park and let our dogs run around while we chatted. In addition to being a talented writer, a gifted seamstress, and an artist, Tammy is an inspired baker. She has gifted this legendary shortbread to me for years. It's utterly decadent. The original recipe is called Millionaire's Shortbread but given that it's so over the top and delicious (and contains a huge amount of butter), we've renamed it Billionaire's Shortbread.

METHOD

SHORTBREAD

Preheat your oven to 350°F. Prepare an 8 × 8-inch baking pan (see page 27).

Sift the flour, baking powder, and salt into the bowl of your stand mixer. Fit your stand mixer with the paddle attachment.

Add the butter and sugar to the bowl of the stand mixer and beat on medium speed until the mixture resembles coarse sand and no large pieces of butter remain, 3–4 minutes. Transfer the mixture to the prepared baking pan and, using your hands or the bottom of a glass, press evenly over the bottom of the pan.

Bake until it begins to turn golden, 10–12 minutes.

Place the pan on a cooling rack to cool completely.

CARAMEL

Increase the oven temperature to 400°F. Combine the butter, condensed milk, and corn syrup in a small saucepan over medium heat and stir until the butter is melted. Add the sugar and stir to combine. Transfer the caramel mixture to a 9 × 13-inch pan (preferably non-stick) with sides at least 2 inches tall. Place the pan on top of a large cookie sheet (to catch any drips that may bubble over) and bake until the caramel is bubbling and

>>

golden, 12–15 minutes. Be sure to stir the caramel a few times with a silicone spatula during baking to prevent too much bubbling over. Remove the caramel from the oven and immediately pour it over the shortbread layer. Smooth the top with an offset spatula, and place in the refrigerator to set for at least 1 hour, or up to overnight.

CHOCOLATE

Combine the chocolate, butter, and corn syrup in a heatproof bowl. Place the bowl over a saucepan of simmering water, making sure the bottom of the bowl is not touching the water. Heat the mixture, stirring occasionally, until melted and smooth.

Pour the chocolate mixture over the caramel layer, using a spatula to smooth the top. Allow to cool for a few minutes, and then sprinkle with coarse salt. Refrigerate for at least 1 hour (but preferably overnight) before slicing.

Use a sharp knife to loosen the edge of the bars from the pan. Using the parchment paper to lift them, remove the bars from the pan and cut into 16 squares.

Trick or Treat Brownies

YIELD: 8 brownies

INGREDIENTS

¼ cup (56 g) unsalted butter
¼ cup (60 ml) vegetable oil
¾ cup (125 g) dark chocolate callets or a good-quality chocolate bar, coarsely chopped
2 Tbsp (17 g) cocoa powder
½ cup + 1 Tbsp (80 g) all-purpose flour
½ tsp salt
¼ tsp baking powder
¾ cup (150 g) sugar
¼ cup (50 g) brown sugar, packed
2 eggs
1 tsp vanilla extract
8–10 snack-sized chocolate bars, chopped into bite-sized chunks
¼ cup (45 g) Smarties (or something similar)

These brownies came about because we had an excess of mini chocolate bars hanging around the bakery after Halloween. We were all eating way too many of them, as you do, and complaining about how impossible they were to resist. But what else could we do? We weren't about to just throw away perfectly good chocolate! Our solution was to chop them up and bake them into a brownie. At the time, I honestly thought it would be a one-off. But customers loved them (especially the Trafalgar school kids who often stop by our Cake Window on their lunch break). So, we bought more mini chocolate bars and kept on baking the Trick or Treat Brownies. They have become one of the most popular items at our Cake Window.

METHOD

Preheat your oven to 350°F. Prepare an 8 × 8-inch baking pan (see page 27).

Place the butter, oil, chocolate, and cocoa powder in a medium-sized heatproof bowl over a saucepan of simmering water, making sure the bottom is not touching the water. Heat, stirring occasionally, until the mixture is melted and smooth. Remove from the heat and set aside for 5 minutes to cool.

Sift the flour, salt, and baking powder into a mixing bowl and set aside.

Add both sugars to the butter/chocolate mixture. Mix to combine and then whisk in the eggs, followed by the vanilla. Fold in the dry ingredients, followed by the chopped-up chocolate bars (do not add the Smarties just yet).

Bake for 12 minutes, remove from the oven, and sprinkle the Smarties evenly over top. Return to the oven and bake until the centre is set and the brownies are slightly pulling away from the edges of the pan, 12–15 minutes.

Remove the pan from the oven and place on a cooling rack. Allow to cool completely before cutting.

This Old House

Epiphany Cakes is located on the ground level of my home on the corner of Stanley and Observatory Streets in Nelson, BC. It's a unique arrangement—a bakery smack-dab in the middle of a residential area—but it seems to work! I love seeing people's expressions of delight and surprise when they happen upon us by accident.

When we moved in, I knew that I wanted to convert the ground-level basement of our new home into a bakery. The house, built in 1898 by Ferguson Pollock (and valued at $850!), had changed hands over twenty times by the time we bought it in 2005. At that point this sweet old place was pretty run-down and in need of a new roof, new windows, new siding, and a new boiler. We moved in with our newborn son, two pugs, and big cat and got to work making improvements and renovating a small section of the unfinished basement to create what would become my bakery.

In the beginning, the bakery was really humble: a household oven purchased second-hand, the white Kitchen Aid mixer I'd purchased while in pastry school, a simple refrigerator, and an ugly linoleum floor. I baked while my son napped. I supplied brownies to Oso Negro and made specialty cakes here and there. As my son grew and I had more time to bake, the bakery grew.

BAKERY
OPEN
9AM-3:30
MON-SAT
closed

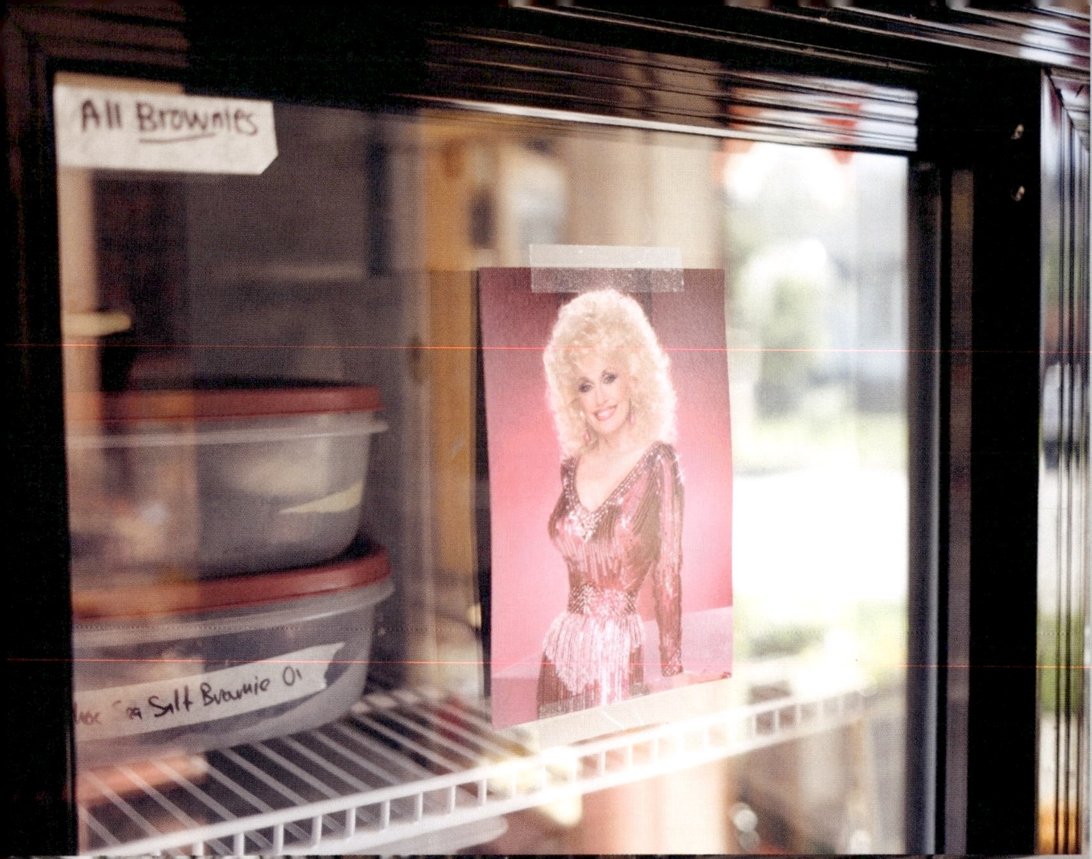
All Brownies
Sea Salt Brownie

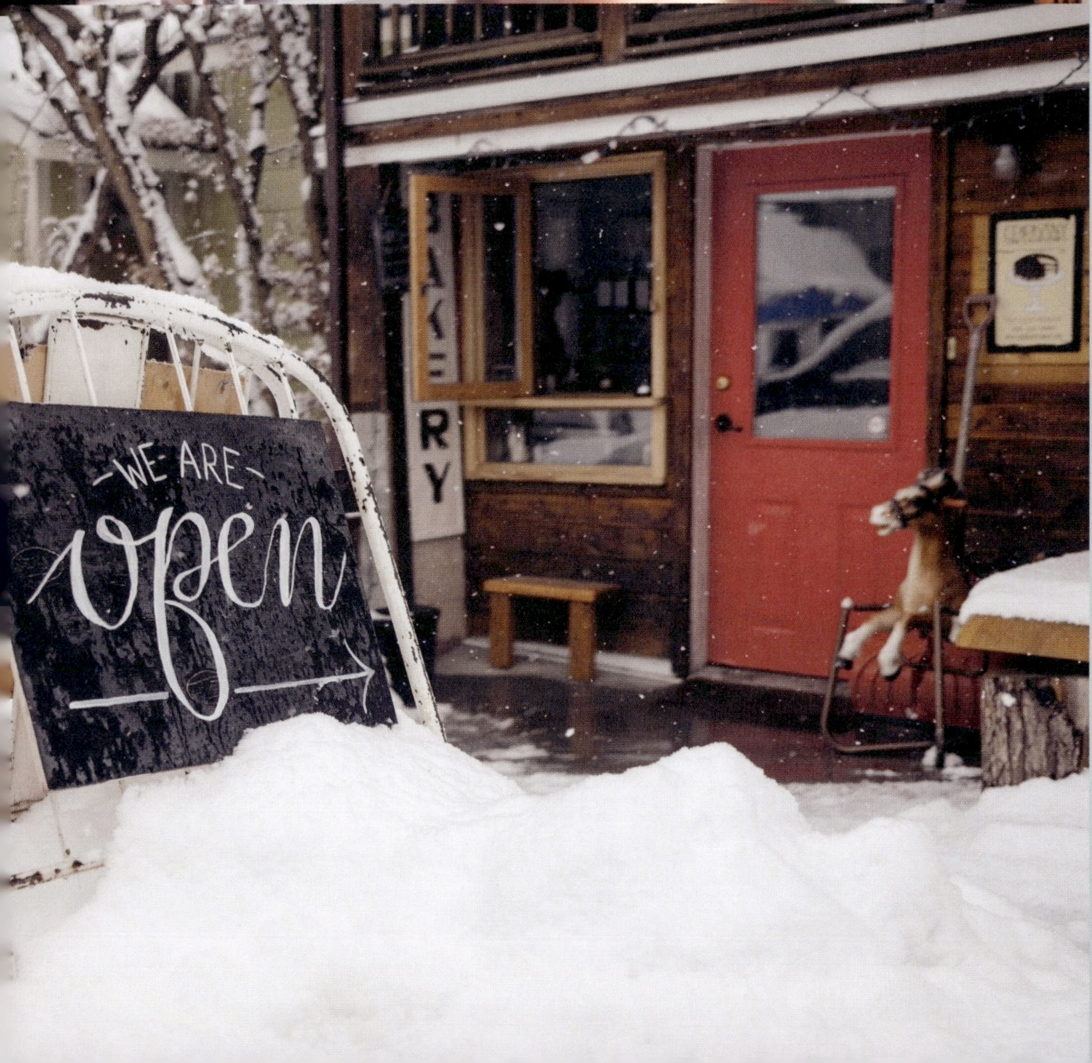
WE ARE
open

Over the years, as the bakery has grown and needed more space, I have finished more of the basement. Epiphany started out as a narrow 200-square-foot galley kitchen. A few years later, it grew to 400 square feet, and it has now expanded into virtually every corner of the ground level of the house.

The space is small but efficient. Since there's no room to accommodate a walk-in cooler, we have lots of individual refrigerators and freezers, which all have names. There's Dolly Parton, Taylor Swift, Leonard Cohen, Eddie Vedder, Mick Jagger, Céline Dion, Justin Bieber, Axl Rose, and George Michael. The names make life easier when someone is looking for something. Rather than saying, "The lemons are in the third fridge in the back," we say, "The lemons are in Justin!" Each fridge has a photo of its namesake taped to the front. Nancy, one of our bakers, affectionately refers to the George Michael fridge as "Georgie," which we all love.

There are, of course, challenges to operating a busy bakery in a house that's over 100 years old. For example, it took over eight hours to manoeuvre our new double-door commercial refrigerator (Dolly) inside the narrow doorway and into a space that was never intended to accommodate commercial-sized kitchen equipment. And we can't receive commercial deliveries at our location, since the semi-truck that brings our baking ingredients cannot come up the steep residential streets that lead to the bakery (we meet the truck behind the Chahko Mika Mall each week to collect our 50-pound bags of cocoa powder and cases of dark chocolate).

The charm of the arrangement far outweighs any of the nuisance of operating from my home—not to mention I'm a total homebody, so working from home suits me just fine. It all makes for a very cozy experience; my staff feel like family, and my son often pops in to grab milk for his cereal or an egg for his breakfast. Outside, my pug, Clementine, happily greets people in front of the bakery, and customers lounge in the sunshine on a wooden bench as the scent of baking wafts out of the window into the neighbourhood. It's all pretty sweet.

I still live above the bakery with my now-teenage son. Sometimes, when I'm sitting on my deck in the summertime, hidden away by laburnum branches, I hear people talking about the bakery as they walk by. Whether they're discovering us for the first time or raving about our cakes, it always makes me smile.

Cookies

59 Gingersnaps

61 Double Chocolate Ginger Chippers

63 Backcountry Cookies

65 Cherry Almond Linzers

67 Tahini Caramel Sandwich Cookies

71 Clemmy's Homemade Dog Treats

72 *The Cake Window*

Gingersnaps

VEGAN
YIELD: 24 cookies

INGREDIENTS

2 cups (280 g) all-purpose flour
1 Tbsp ground ginger
2 tsp baking soda
1 tsp ground cinnamon
½ tsp salt
¼ tsp ground cloves
¾ cup (170 g) unsalted plant-based butter
1 cup (200 g) brown sugar, packed
1 tsp vanilla extract
¼ cup (90 g) organic blackstrap molasses
¼ cup (60 ml) organic soy milk
½ cup (100 g) sugar, for rolling the cookies

NOTE: If you don't have a scoop, or prefer to roll the cookies by hand, aim to make each one about the size of a golf ball.

Given the choice between a chewy cookie and a crispy cookie, I will always vote chewy! We use organic blackstrap molasses in our gingersnaps, which makes these cookies deliciously moist and soft, just the way I like 'em.

METHOD

Preheat your oven to 350°F. Line two (13 × 18-inch) cookie sheets with parchment paper.

Sift the flour, ground ginger, baking soda, cinnamon, salt, and cloves into a bowl and set aside.

Place the plant-based butter, sugar, and vanilla in the bowl of a stand mixer. Fit your stand mixer with the paddle attachment and beat on medium speed until light and fluffy, about 2 minutes, scraping down the sides of the bowl as needed. Add the molasses and milk and continue to mix until fully combined.

Add the dry ingredients to the bowl and mix on medium speed until fully combined and there are no streaks of flour visible.

Place the ½ cup (100 g) of sugar in a small bowl. Use a (2 Tbsp) scoop to portion balls of dough, and then drop each one into the bowl of sugar to coat completely. Place the cookies on the baking trays about 1 inch apart. They will spread while baking.

Bake until the edges are firm, and the tops are cracked, 12–14 minutes. Place the pans on a cooling rack. Allow the cookies to cool completely before transferring to an airtight container.

Double Chocolate Ginger Chippers

VEGAN, GLUTEN-FREE
YIELD: 15 bite-sized cookies

These Chipper Cookies are all that remain from a brief flirtation I had with the paleo diet several years ago. I developed them because I needed a naturally sweetened high protein treat. My commitment to the paleo lifestyle didn't last, but my love of these cookies is still going strong. They are delicious and satisfying—and popular with our customers, who love that they are both gluten-free and vegan.

INGREDIENTS

⅓ cup (70 ml) coconut oil
¼ cup (40 g) candied ginger
2 cups (200 g) ground almonds
¼ cup (34 g) cocoa powder, sifted
¼ tsp salt
½ tsp baking soda
¼ cup (60 ml) pure maple syrup
1 tsp vanilla extract
¼ cup (42 g) vegan dark chocolate chips

NOTES:

— If you're not a fan of candied ginger, you can replace it with the same volume/weight of dried cranberries or just double up on the chocolate chips.
— If you don't have a scoop, or you prefer to roll the cookies by hand, aim to make each one about the size of a golf ball.

METHOD

Preheat your oven to 350°F. Line a (13 × 18-inch) cookie sheet with parchment paper.

Place the coconut oil in a saucepan on low heat until just melted. Cool the coconut oil until it's lukewarm but still pourable.

Chop the candied ginger into pea-sized pieces.

Place the ground almonds, cocoa powder, salt, and baking soda in a medium bowl. Mix to combine and then add the coconut oil. Mix well and then add the maple syrup and vanilla. Finally, fold in the chocolate chips and ginger.

Use a (2 Tbsp/30 ml) scoop to shape the cookies into small balls. Place them on the cookie sheet about 1 inch apart. They will hold their shape and will not spread much.

Bake until firm to the touch, about 15 minutes.

Place the pan on a cooling rack. Allow the cookies to cool completely before transferring to an airtight container. Store the cookies in the refrigerator.

Backcountry Cookies

VEGAN
YIELD: 16 cookies

INGREDIENTS

- ½ cup (70 g) organic sunflower seeds
- 1 cup (150 g) organic spelt flour
- 1 tsp ground cinnamon
- ¾ cup (80 g) quick oats
- ½ cup (75 g) organic pumpkin seeds
- 2 Tbsp organic ground flax seeds
- ¼ cup (25 g) unsweetened shredded coconut
- ¾ cup (115 g) sultana raisins
- ½ cup (125 ml) soy milk
- ⅓ cup (80 ml) vegetable oil
- 2 Tbsp blackstrap molasses
- 2 Tbsp water
- ½ cup (100 g) brown sugar, packed
- 2 tsp vanilla extract
- ¾ cup (125 g) vegan dark chocolate chips

Folks in the Kootenays take their outdoor adventuring very seriously. Winters are spent flying down the slopes at our local ski hill or gliding along cross-country ski trails. Summers are spent beaching, camping, biking, hiking, and floating down the Slocan River. No matter what the activity, these cookies are the perfect power-snack to take along. It's no surprise that these are our most popular cookies—we sell thousands of them a year. Packed with raisins, dark chocolate, oats, molasses, and seeds, they're healthy, hearty, and delicious. In addition, they are vegan and nut-free, making them a perfect treat for kids' lunchboxes as well.

METHOD

Preheat your oven to 350°F. Line two (13 × 18-inch) cookie sheets with parchment paper.

Place the sunflower seeds on one of the cookie sheets and toast them in the oven until fragrant, 5–7 minutes. Set aside to cool on the pan.

Combine the cooled sunflower seeds, the flour, cinnamon, oats, pumpkin seeds, flax seeds, shredded coconut, and raisins in a large bowl.

Place the soy milk, oil, molasses, water, sugar, and vanilla in another large bowl and whisk to combine. Add the dry ingredients to the wet ingredients and fold to combine. Fold in the chocolate chips.

Use a (2 Tbsp/30 ml) scoop to place 16 scoops of dough on the prepared cookies sheets, about 2 inches apart. Place a piece of parchment paper over each cookie and flatten using the bottom of a glass. Once flattened, there should be about ½ inch between each cookie. They won't spread very much.

Bake the cookies until they are fragrant and no longer shiny, about 15 minutes.

Place the pans on a cooling rack. Allow the cookies to cool completely before transferring to an airtight container for storage.

Cherry Almond Linzers

YIELD: 16 sandwich cookies

INGREDIENTS

LINZER DOUGH

1½ cups (210 g) all-purpose flour
1½ cups (150 g) ground almonds
¼ tsp salt
¼ tsp ground cloves
¼ tsp ground cinnamon
½ cup (113 g) unsalted butter, at room temperature
½ cup (100 g) sugar
1 large egg, at room temperature
2 tsp vanilla extract

FILLING

½ cup (150 g) cherry jam

NOTES:

— I have found that these cookies taste best the day after they're filled with jam, which gives everything a chance to meld together.

— If you don't have 2½-inch and 1-inch cookie cutters on hand, any combination of a large cookie cutter plus a smaller cookie cutter will do.

— Cherry jam is my favourite filling, but you can fill these cookies with any kind of jam you like!

These cookies are popular at our Cake Window around the winter holidays. We also include them in our holiday cookie boxes. The combination of cloves and ground almonds creates a deliciously fragrant cookie. The dough does not need to be chilled before rolling, so these cookies come together in under an hour.

METHOD

LINZER DOUGH

Preheat your oven to 350°F. Line two (13 × 18-inch) cookie sheets with parchment paper.

Sift the flour, almonds, salt, cloves, and cinnamon into a mixing bowl and set aside.

Fit your stand mixer with the paddle attachment. Place the butter and sugar in the bowl of the stand mixer. Beat on high speed until light and fluffy, about 3 minutes. Add the egg, followed by the vanilla, and continue to beat until combined. Add the dry ingredients and beat on low speed just until the dough comes together.

Transfer the dough to a floured work surface, cut it in half, and form each piece into a ball. Working with one ball of dough at a time, roll out to ⅛-inch thickness with a rolling pin.

Cut 32 cookies using a 2½-inch round cookie cutter. Gather up the scraps and re-roll as necessary. Use a 1-inch cookie cutter to cut a window into 16 of the cookies. Transfer the cookies to the prepared cookie sheets, leaving ½ inch of space between each one. Bake until they're just turning golden, about 10 minutes.

Place the pan on a cooling rack and allow to cool completely.

FILLING AND ASSEMBLY

Once the cookies are cool, place a dollop of jam on the centre of each of the cookies without a window cut-out. Spread the jam to the edge of each cookie using an offset spatula and place a cookie with the window cut-out on top to create a sandwich.

Tahini Caramel Sandwich Cookies

YIELD: 36 sandwich cookies

INGREDIENTS

CARAMEL FILLING

½ batch Salted Caramel (page 210)

COOKIES

1 cup (227 g) unsalted butter
1 cup (130 g) icing sugar
2¼ cups (315 g) all-purpose flour
¾ cup (100 g) cocoa powder, plus more for the countertop
½ tsp salt
¼ cup (60 ml) milk
2 tsp vanilla extract

TAHINI FILLING

¼ cup (57 g) unsalted butter, at room temperature
⅓ cup (43 g) icing sugar, sifted
½ cup (125g) tahini
½ tsp vanilla extract

I find sandwich cookies so nostalgic and fun, and there's something about making your own sandwich cookies that feels extra special. I'm also a huge fan of tahini. I love it because it reminds me of growing up in the Middle East and adds a surprising hit of savoury umami flavour to baked goods. I use it in my baking every chance I get.

METHOD

CARAMEL FILLING

Prepare the caramel according to the recipe instructions. Let it cool while you prepare the cookie dough and tahini filling.

COOKIES

Place the butter in the bowl of a stand mixer. Sift in the icing sugar, fit your mixer with the paddle attachment, and beat on low speed until combined, 2–3 minutes.

Sift the flour, cocoa powder, and salt into the mixing bowl. Mix on low speed until no streaks of flour remain. Add the milk and vanilla and mix until just combined.

Dust the countertop with some flour. Transfer the dough (it might still look a bit crumbly at this point) to the countertop and continue to work it with your hands until it comes together. Divide the dough into two pieces. Wrap each piece in plastic wrap and refrigerate for at least 1 hour, or up to overnight.

Line two (9 × 13-inch) cookie sheets with parchment paper.

Dust the countertop with cocoa powder and work one block of dough at a time with your hands until it's warm enough to roll. Roll the dough out to ¼-inch thick (be sure to move the dough around from time to time so it doesn't stick to the counter). Use a 2-inch cookie cutter to cut out the cookies and place them on a cookie sheet, about 1 inch apart. Repeat with the second block of dough. Refrigerate for at least 20 minutes before baking.

Preheat your oven to 350°F.

Bake the cookies until the edges are firm and the tops are no longer shiny, 10–12 minutes.

>>

Place the cookie sheets onto a cooling rack. Allow the cookies to cool while you prepare the filling.

NOTE: You will have some leftover caramel from this recipe. You can store it in the refrigerator for up to a week and reheat it when you're ready to use it. A few ideas for how to use up leftover caramel: stir it into your hot coffee, make an iced caramel latte, make a Salted Caramel Cake (page 129), drizzle it over ice cream, or prepare a batch of Our Classic Brownies (page 41) and swirl it into the batter before baking.

TAHINI FILLING

Place the butter and icing sugar in the bowl of a stand mixer. Fit your mixer with the paddle attachment and beat on medium speed until light and fluffy, 3–5 minutes. Add the tahini and vanilla and mix until combined. Transfer the tahini icing to a piping bag fitted with a small round piping tip.

ASSEMBLY

Turn half of the cookies over so that the underside is facing up. Pipe a ring of tahini filling around the edge of the cookies, fill the centre with about ½ teaspoon of caramel. Resist the urge to overfill the cookies, otherwise they'll be messy to eat. Place a second cookie on top of the filling to complete the sandwich. Place the cookies on a clean cookie sheet and chill, uncovered, for about 30 minutes before you enjoy.

Clemmy's Homemade Dog Treats

YIELD: 50 (3-inch, bone-shaped) dog biscuits

INGREDIENTS

⅔ cup (150 g) pumpkin purée (be sure to use pumpkin purée, not pumpkin pie filling)
½ cup (125 g) organic smooth peanut butter
2 eggs
1 cup (150g) spelt flour, plus more for rolling
½ cup (75 g) brown rice flour
½ cup (50 g) quick oats

NOTE: Please read the label on your peanut butter carefully, as some peanut butter contains xylitol, which is harmful to dogs.

If you've ever visited our Cake Window, you'll know that we LOVE dogs! We always have homemade dog treats on hand for our furry friends, and if the sun is out, our resident pug, Clementine, is sure to be lounging outside of the bakery greeting customers.

These treats are very cute if you use a dog-bone-shaped cookie cutter (If you don't have a dog-bone cookie cutter, don't worry about it. Any small cookie cutter will do.)

METHOD

Preheat your oven to 350°F. Line two (13 × 18-inch) cookie sheets with parchment paper.

Place the pumpkin purée, peanut butter, and eggs in a large bowl and mix until smooth. Using a silicone spatula, fold in the flours and oats and continue to fold until the dough comes together.

Turn the dough onto a floured work surface and roll it out into a disk about ¼-inch thick. Using your cookie cutter, cut out cookies and place on the prepared baking tray lined with parchment paper. Gather up the leftover bits of dough and roll out again until you've used all the dough up. The biscuits do not spread much, so space them about ½-inch apart on the baking sheet.

Bake until "bone" dry (sorry, I couldn't resist), 35–40 minutes.

Place the cookie sheets on a cooling rack. Allow the biscuits to cool completely before storing in an airtight container. They will keep for several weeks.

The Cake Window

In 2020 we added a beautiful locally crafted wooden take-out window to the bakery's front facade. We dubbed it the Cake Window and started selling brownies, cookies, cupcakes, and cake slices out of it (prior to 2020, we were a wholesale and special-order-only operation).

The Cake Window has given us the opportunity to interact more with our customers and be a more active part of the community—and we love it. Neighbours stop by for a cookie-fix, friends cruise by on their e-bikes for brownies, tourists discover us while exploring Nelson's scenic streets, Trafalgar middle-school kids swing by on their lunch breaks, and local dogs pull their owners here on their daily walks (this might be because we give a homemade dog treat to every dog that visits the bakery).

OPEN
9AM-3:30
MON-SAT

Simple Cakes & Loaves

77 Chocolate Peanut Butter Slab Cake

79 Epiphany Chocolate Slab Cake with Ganache Glaze

81 Cake-ettes with Whipped Cream and Berries

83 Chocolate Quinoa Cake

87 Vanilla Funfetti Cupcakes with Cream Cheese Icing

89 Vegan Carrot Cake

91 Olive Oil Cake with Rose Syrup, Strawberries, and Mascarpone Cream

93 Lemon Poppyseed Bundt Cake with White Chocolate Glaze

97 Chocolate Bundt Cake with Ganache Glaze

101 Brown Butter Rice Krispie Cake

103 Chocolate Cake with Luscious Milk Chocolate Icing

107 Loaded Cardamom Banana Bread

109 Lemon Almond Loaf

111 Chocolate Zucchini Loaf

112 *Jacinta Sousa, Friend & Neighbour*

Chocolate Peanut Butter Slab Cake

YIELD: 8 servings

INGREDIENTS

CAKE

1 Epiphany Chocolate Cake (page 191)

PEANUT BUTTER ICING

⅓ cup (43 g) icing sugar
¼ cup (56 g) unsalted butter, at room temperature
½ cup (125 g) smooth peanut butter
1 tsp vanilla extract

GARNISH (OPTIONAL)

Candied Peanuts (page 217), for sprinkling

NOTE: This recipe only requires a handful of candied peanuts, so if you choose to make the garnish you will end up with extra candied nuts to snack on.

Shortly after graduating from pastry school, I worked at a cake shop called Sweet Obsession in Vancouver. I learned a lot there, baking and decorating a huge selection of fancy cakes, my favourite of which was their silky decadent Peanut Butter Chocolate Mousse Cake. Chocolate and peanut butter remains one of my all-time favourite flavour combos. When I started my own bakery, I knew I had to have a chocolate peanut butter cake on the menu. This cake combines moist chocolate cake, creamy peanut butter icing, and an irresistible sweet/salty candied peanut garnish.

METHOD

CAKE

Prepare the chocolate cake, following the instructions for the slab cake.

Once the cake has cooled completely, prepare the icing.

PEANUT BUTTER ICING

Sift the icing sugar into the bowl of a stand mixer. Fit your mixer with the paddle attachment, add the butter, and begin beating on low speed. Once the sugar has been absorbed a bit—just enough that it won't fly out of the bowl—turn the mixer up to medium speed and beat until light and fluffy, 3–5 minutes, scraping down the sides of the bowl as needed.

Add the peanut butter and the vanilla. Beat on medium speed until fully combined and smooth.

ASSEMBLY

Spread the icing onto the cooled cake using an offset spatula to create swirls. Sprinkle the cake with candied peanuts if using.

Epiphany Chocolate Slab Cake with Ganache Glaze

YIELD: 8 servings

INGREDIENTS

CAKE

1 Epiphany Chocolate Cake (page 191)

GANACHE GLAZE

1½ cups (250 g) dark chocolate callets

1 cup (250 ml) whipping cream

NOTE: The leftover ganache can be collected, stored in an airtight container in the refrigerator or freezer, and reheated later for another use. See page 205 for instructions on how to use ganache to make truffles or hot cocoa.

This is my favourite kind of cake because it looks super-fancy but it's quite simple to make. Ganache has a way of easily elevating the look of baked goods with its shiny, elegant finish. Level up by sprinkling the top with fresh berries. They look amazing and taste scrumptious when paired with the dark chocolate ganache glaze.

METHOD

CAKE

Prepare the chocolate cake, following the instructions for the slab cake on page 191.

Once the cake has cooled completely, prepare your ganache.

GANACHE GLAZE

Prepare the ganache glaze following the instructions on page 205.

ASSEMBLY

Flip the cooled cake over so that the domed side is facing up.

Place the cake on a cooling rack. Place the cooling rack on top of a large bowl or cookie sheet. Pour the ganache over the cake, letting the excess drip into the bowl or cookie sheet below. Place the cake, still on the cooling rack, in the refrigerator for about 10–15 minutes to allow the ganache to set.

Once the glaze has set, remove the cake from the cooling rack, transfer to a cake plate, and store in the refrigerator until ready to serve.

Cake-ettes with Whipped Cream and Berries

GLUTEN-FREE
YIELD: 6 cake-ettes

These little cakes pack a serious punch. The combination of chocolate and butter creates a dense, delicious cake that's offset perfectly by the lightness of the whipped cream and berries.

INGREDIENTS

CAKE-ETTES

1 cup (170 g) dark chocolate callets or a good-quality chocolate bar, coarsely chopped
¾ cup (170 g) unsalted butter
1 cup (200 g) sugar
¼ cup (35 g) gluten-free flour blend
1 tsp salt
5 eggs
1 tsp vanilla extract

WHIPPED CREAM

¾ cup (180 ml) whipping cream
1 tsp vanilla extract
¼ cup (32 g) icing sugar

GARNISH

Fresh raspberries
Icing sugar

METHOD

CAKE-ETTES

Preheat your oven to 350°F. Prepare a jumbo muffin pan (see note) by spraying the cups with pan spray (no need to use paper cupcake liners for this recipe).

Place the chocolate and butter in a heatproof bowl over a pan of simmering water, making sure the bottom is not touching the water. Stir occasionally. When the mixture is completely melted and smooth, remove from the heat, mix in the sugar, and set aside to cool completely, 10–15 minutes.

Sift the flour and salt into a small bowl. Place the eggs and vanilla in another small bowl and whisk to combine.

When the chocolate mixture is cool but still liquid, whisk in the eggs and vanilla. Fold in the flour and salt. Divide the batter evenly between the cups of the muffin pan.

Bake until the cakes are puffed and the outsides are set, about 30 minutes (the centres may still be a bit liquidy—that's okay, they will set as they cool). Remove from the oven and place the pan on a cooling rack. Cool the cakes completely before removing them from the pan.

WHIPPED CREAM

Once your cakes are cool, place the whipping cream, vanilla, and icing sugar in the bowl of a stand mixer. Fit your stand mixer with the whisk attachment. Whip the cream until medium peaks form (the cream holds its shape well, but the tip of the peaks curl slightly when the beater is lifted).

>>

NOTES:

- The cake-ettes can be made several days in advance and stored in the refrigerator in an airtight container. Serve them at room temperature and top with whipped cream just before serving.

ASSEMBLY

Flip each cake-ette over so that the bottom side is facing up. Top with a dusting of icing sugar, a dollop of whipped cream, and fresh berries.

Chocolate Quinoa Cake

GLUTEN-FREE, DAIRY-FREE
YIELD: 10–12 servings

INGREDIENTS

CAKE

1 cup (135 g) cocoa powder
1½ tsp baking powder
½ tsp baking soda
½ tsp salt
4 eggs
¾ cup (180 ml) vegetable oil
⅓ cup (80 ml) full-fat coconut milk
2 tsp vanilla extract
2 cups (300 g) cooked organic white quinoa (see note)
1½ cups (300 g) sugar

DAIRY-FREE GANACHE GLAZE

1 cup (250 ml) full-fat coconut milk
1½ cups (250 g) dark chocolate callets
1 tsp coconut oil

GARNISH (OPTIONAL)

Fresh blueberries

Several years ago, my neighbour Francyne loaned me a cookbook called *Quinoa 365* by Patricia Green and Carolyn Hemming, where I came across a recipe for a chocolate cake made with quinoa. The recipe calls for cooking quinoa and blending it into a batter, resulting in a cake that's deliciously moist and gluten-free. I immediately loved the idea of making a cake using quinoa instead of flour, and I was inspired to create something similar for our customers. People go crazy for this cake's dense texture and luxurious dairy-free ganache glaze.

METHOD

CAKE

Preheat your oven to 350°F. Prepare an 8-inch round × 3-inch tall cake pan (see page 27).

Sift the cocoa powder, baking powder, baking soda, and salt into a medium bowl and set aside.

Place the eggs, oil, milk, and vanilla in a blender. Add the quinoa and blend until completely smooth.

Transfer the mixture to a mixing bowl and use a silicone spatula to fold in the sugar, followed by the rest of the dry ingredients.

Transfer the batter to the prepared baking pan and bake until a knife inserted in the centre of the cake comes out mostly clean, 40–50 minutes (there may be a few wet crumbs on the knife; that's fine, as long as the cake itself is set.)

Place the pan on a cooling rack. Allow the cake to cool completely before removing from the pan. This cake has no gluten, so it will be quite fragile and prone to breaking while it's warm. Handle with care.

>>

NOTES:

- To make 2 cups (300 g) of cooked quinoa, place ½ cup (80 g) dry quinoa into a saucepan with 1 cup (250 ml) water. Bring to a boil, turn down the heat to low, cover, and cook until all the water is absorbed, and the quinoa is tender, 10 minutes. Allow the quinoa to cool completely before using.
- A high-powered blender works best for this recipe, but a regular blender or food processor can get the job done too. Just be sure that all the quinoa is well-blended and the batter is smooth.

DAIRY-FREE GANACHE GLAZE

Once the cake is completely cool, prepare the dairy-free ganache glaze. Place the coconut milk into a saucepan and bring to a simmer. Place the chocolate into a bowl with the coconut oil. Pour the coconut milk into the bowl with the chocolate and allow to stand without stirring for 5 minutes. Whisk until smooth and then allow the ganache to cool at room temperature for 10–15 minutes.

ASSEMBLY

Remove the cooled cake from the pan and place it on a cooling rack. Place the cooling rack over a large bowl or a cookie sheet. Pour the ganache over the cake, allowing the excess to fall into the bowl or tray below. Place the cake, still on the cooling rack, in the refrigerator for 10–15 minutes, just long enough to allow the ganache to set.

Use an offset spatula to carefully transfer the cake to a serving plate. Top the cake with fresh blueberries (if using). They pair beautifully with the colour and the flavour of the dark chocolate in this cake. If not serving immediately, store the cake in the refrigerator.

CUPCAKE VARIATION

YIELD: 24 cupcakes

Preheat your oven to 350°F. Line the cups of two muffin pans with 24 cupcake liners.

Prepare the batter as described above. Use the (¼ cup/60ml) scoop to fill each cup three-quarters full and bake until a knife inserted into the centre of a cupcake comes out clean, about 20 minutes.

Place the cupcakes on a cooling rack to cool completely before removing them from the pan and decorating with Aquafaba Vanilla Icing (page 203) or your icing of choice.

Vanilla Funfetti Cupcakes with Cream Cheese Icing

YIELD: 16 cupcakes

INGREDIENTS

1½ cups (187 g) cake flour
2 tsp baking powder
½ tsp salt
½ cup (113 g) unsalted butter, melted and slightly cooled
1 cup (200 g) sugar
2 tsp vanilla extract
2 egg whites
½ cup (125 ml) milk
½ cup (125 ml) full-fat sour cream
¼ cup (40 g) rainbow sprinkles, plus more for decorating
1 batch Cream Cheese Icing (page 204)

NOTE: It's important to use cake flour, not all-purpose flour, for this recipe. Cake flour contains less gluten, is ground extra-fine, and creates a tender crumb, making it an ideal choice for vanilla cakes. If you can't find cake flour, or you can roughly replicate its effects by using all-purpose flour and cornstarch as follows: For every 1 cup of cake flour in your recipe, measure out 1 cup of all-purpose flour, remove 2 tablespoons, and replace them with 2 tablespoons of cornstarch.

Is there anything more festive than a funfetti cupcake? I think not! From 2008 until 2018 I was a vendor at Market Fest, a popular night market on Baker Street in downtown Nelson. Rain or shine, my friend Sarah and I would set up our tent, string it with fairy lights, pile our table high with cupcakes, cookies, and Sarah's famous peach pies, and then stand back and enjoy the scene. The Moving Mosaic Samba Band would always kick off the evening, marching past in a cacophony of sound and colour, followed closely by streams of locals and tourists admiring the booths showcasing handmade ceramics, jewellery, local produce, textiles, and food. These cupcakes were always a popular item at those markets.

METHOD

Preheat your oven to 350°F. Line two muffin pans with 16 paper cupcake liners.

Sift the flour, baking powder, and salt into a medium bowl.

In another medium bowl, whisk together the melted butter, sugar, vanilla, and egg whites until light and fluffy. Combine the milk and sour cream.

Alternate adding the dry ingredients and the milk and sour cream mixture, using a silicone spatula to fold in each addition, beginning and ending with the dry ingredients. Do not overmix. Finally, fold in the sprinkles.

Scoop the batter into the prepared muffin pans. I use a (¼ cup/60 ml) scoop to ensure evenly sized cupcakes. Place the muffin pan on a cookie sheet (to prevent the bottoms of the cupcakes from browning too much), and bake until lightly golden and a knife inserted in the centre of a cupcake comes out clean, 15–18 minutes.

Prepare the cream cheese icing.

When the cupcakes are completely cool, decorate them with cream cheese icing and more sprinkles.

Vegan Carrot Cake

VEGAN
YIELD: 8 servings

INGREDIENTS

1 cup (200 g) sugar
1 cup (250 ml) full-fat coconut milk
½ cup (125 ml) vegetable oil
½ cup (125 ml) unsweetened apple sauce (the little pre-packaged snack cups of apple sauce work well here)
2 tsp vanilla extract
2 cups (200 g) grated organic carrots (2–3 medium carrots)
2¼ cups (315 g) all-purpose flour
1 Tbsp baking powder
1 tsp baking soda
1 tsp salt
2 tsp ground cinnamon
1 tsp ground ginger
½ tsp ground nutmeg
½ batch Aquafaba Vanilla Icing (page 203)

NOTE: This recipe can also be used to make a layer cake. Divide the batter evenly between three 8-inch cake pans. Bake the cakes until a knife inserted in the centre comes out clean and the cakes are pulling away slightly from the edges of the pans, 15–20 minutes. Decorate with Aquafaba Vanilla Icing (see page 121 for tips on how to decorate a layer cake).

We work hard to create delicious cakes for folks with dietary restrictions. Our goal is for our vegan, dairy-free, and gluten-free cakes to be just as tasty as everything else that we bake. Based on our customers' feedback, I think we have succeeded. We make three kinds of carrot cake at Epiphany: classic (page 141), gluten-free (page 145), and vegan. They all get rave reviews. We use organic carrots in all of our carrot cakes. I believe that you can taste the difference.

METHOD

Preheat your oven to 350°F. Prepare an 8 × 8-inch baking pan (see page 27).

Place the sugar, coconut milk, oil, apple sauce, and vanilla in a large bowl and whisk to combine. Use a silicone spatula to fold in the grated carrots.

Sift the flour, baking powder, baking soda, salt, and spices into the bowl with the carrot mixture and fold gently until well combined and no streaks of flour are visible.

Transfer the batter to the prepared baking pan.

Bake until a knife inserted in the centre of the cake comes out clean, 40–45 minutes.

Place the pan on a cooling rack. Allow the cake to cool completely before removing from the pan and decorating with the icing.

Olive Oil Cake with Rose Syrup, Strawberries, and Mascarpone Cream

YIELD: 10–12 servings

INGREDIENTS

CAKE

- 1½ cups (210 g) all-purpose flour
- 1 tsp baking powder
- ¼ tsp salt
- ½ cup (125 ml) full-fat milk
- 1 tsp vanilla extract
- 1 cup (200 g) sugar
- ½ cup (125 ml) extra virgin olive oil
- 2 eggs
- 2 egg yolks
- 1 cup (150 g) sliced fresh strawberries, for garnish

ROSE SYRUP

- ½ cup (15 g) organic dried rose petals
- ½ cup (100 g) sugar
- ½ cup (125 ml) water

MASCARPONE CREAM

- ½ cup (137 g) mascarpone cheese
- ¼ cup (32 g) icing sugar
- 1 cup (250 ml) whipping cream
- 1 tsp vanilla extract

NOTE: Mascarpone cheese can be pricey. If you prefer, you can use whipped cream without the mascarpone. It will still be delicious.

I love olive oil, and there's something about olive oil in a cake that really speaks to me. When I was a kid, my family used to spend time in Greece with my parents' best friends, Yiannis and Georgia. I have a lot of wonderful childhood memories of our time spent in Yiannis's familial village of Raches in the Peloponnese, an area famous for olive oil production. When we visited there I spent hours wandering around by myself in the olive groves (it was the eighties!), climbing trees, picking wildflowers, chatting with goats, and catching tadpoles. The combination of olive oil and roses in this cake takes me back to that magical time.

METHOD

CAKE

Preheat your oven to 350°F. Prepare an 8-inch round × 3-inch tall cake pan (see page 27).

Sift the flour, baking powder, and salt into a small bowl and set aside.

Combine the milk and vanilla in a measuring cup.

Place the sugar and oil in the bowl of a stand mixer. Fit the mixer with the whisk attachment and beat on medium speed until combined. Add the eggs, one at a time, followed by the yolks. Increase the mixer speed to high and beat until the mixture is pale and thickened, 1–2 minutes.

Stop the mixer and add the dry ingredients to the batter, mix to combine, and then add the milk and vanilla. Do not overmix.

Transfer the batter to the prepared cake pan. Bake until the cake is turning golden, and a knife inserted in the centre comes out clean, 30–40 minutes.

Place the pan on a cooling rack until the cake is cool enough to handle—about 10 minutes—and then turn out onto the cooling rack to cool completely.

>>

ROSE SYRUP

Place the rose petals, sugar, and water in a small saucepan. Stir to combine and bring to a simmer over medium heat. Simmer, stirring occasionally, until the sugar has dissolved, about 6–8 minutes, and then remove from the heat. Set the syrup aside to cool and infuse for 30 minutes.

MASCARPONE CREAM

Place the mascarpone cheese, icing sugar, cream, and vanilla in the bowl of a stand mixer. Fit the mixer with the whisk attachment and whip on high speed until stiff peaks form, 1–3 minutes.

Place the bowl in the refrigerator until you are ready to assemble the cake.

ASSEMBLY

Strain the syrup into a measuring cup (use the back of a spoon to press all the liquid out of the rose petals before discarding them). Place the cooled cake back in the cake pan and prick the top of the cake in several places with a fork. Pour the rose syrup over the cake and allow it to soak in for a few minutes.

Remove the cake from the pan and transfer it to a serving plate. Top with the mascarpone cream and sliced strawberries.

Lemon Poppyseed Bundt Cake with White Chocolate Glaze

YIELD: 12 servings

INGREDIENTS

CAKE

⅔ cup (160 ml) milk, divided
¼ cup (60 ml) vegetable oil
2 tsp vanilla extract
1 tsp lemon extract
5 eggs
3 cups (450 g) light spelt flour
2 cups (400 g) sugar
1 Tbsp baking powder
½ tsp salt
1 cup (227 g) unsalted butter, at room temperature
Zest of 1 organic lemon
2–3 Tbsp lemon juice
¼ cup (35 g) poppy seeds

GLAZE

½ cup (100 g) good-quality white chocolate
¼ cup + 1 Tbsp (75 ml) whipping cream

This cake is close to my heart. If you read the intro to this book, you'll know that a lemon poppyseed cake made me fall in love with baking and changed the course of my life, so it's a pretty big deal!

METHOD

CAKE

Combine ⅓ cup (80 ml) of the milk with the oil, vanilla, and lemon extract in a small bowl or measuring cup.

Mix the other ⅓ cup of the milk with the eggs in a separate small bowl. Set all the liquid ingredients aside for 40–60 minutes to come to room temperature.

Preheat your oven to 350°F. Prepare a 9-inch Bundt pan (see page 27).

Sift the flour, sugar, baking powder, and salt into the bowl of your stand mixer. Fit the mixer with the paddle attachment. Add the butter and lemon zest and beat on medium speed until well mixed, about 1 minute.

Add the milk/oil mixture and beat on medium speed for exactly 2 minutes (this step is to fully coat the flour in butter, which limits gluten development, creating a dense cake with a tender crumb).

Scrape down the sides of the mixer and the paddle using a silicone spatula and then, with the mixer running on low speed, add the milk/egg mixture. Turn the mixer speed up to medium and beat until a smooth batter forms. Scrape down the sides of the mixer and the paddle again if necessary. Add the lemon juice and poppy seeds and mix on low speed until just combined.

Transfer the batter to the prepared Bundt pan and bake until a knife inserted in the cake comes out clean, about 40 minutes. Place the pan on a cooling rack until the cake is cool enough to handle—about 10 minutes—and then turn it out onto the cooling rack to cool completely.

>>

GLAZE

Place the chocolate in a heatproof bowl. Place the cream in a small saucepan over low heat, bring to a simmer and pour it over the chocolate. Allow to stand for 2–3 minutes and then whisk until smooth. Allow the glaze to cool for 20 minutes until cool and thick, but still pourable. If it's too warm when you pour it on, it will be opaque and roll right off the cake.

ASSEMBLY

Place the cooling rack with the cake on it over a cookie sheet. Pour the glaze over the cake, allowing any excess glaze to fall onto the tray below. Place the cake in the refrigerator to allow the glaze to set completely, about 30 minutes. Use an offset spatula to transfer it to a cake plate.

Chocolate Bundt Cake with Ganache Glaze

YIELD: 12 servings

INGREDIENTS

CAKE

1 cup (140 g) all-purpose flour
⅓ cup (45 g) cocoa powder
1 tsp baking soda
1 tsp baking powder
½ tsp salt
½ cup (50 g) quick oats
1 cup (250 ml) boiling water
½ cup (113 g) unsalted butter
1½ cups (300 g) brown sugar, packed
2 eggs
1 tsp vanilla extract

GANACHE GLAZE

½ cup (125 ml) whipping cream
¾ cup (125 g) dark chocolate callets

I came across this oatmeal cake in the first Whitewater Cooks cookbook. Whitewater is the name of our local ski hill, which also happens to have excellent food and is the inspiration for several popular cookbooks written by Shelley Adams. Shelley is a local legend. I used to run into her hiking Pulpit Rock (a popular, very steep 1.7-kilometre local hike) and always felt a bit intimidated crossing paths with such a local celebrity. I had the opportunity to get to know her when I made a cake for her son's wedding in 2023. She has generously given me advice throughout the process of writing this book—and permission to share the recipe for her Chocolate Oatmeal Cake. I've adapted her recipe slightly by making it a Bundt cake and adding a chocolate glaze.

METHOD

CAKE

Preheat your oven to 350°F. Prepare a 9-inch Bundt pan (see page 27).

Sift the flour, cocoa powder, baking soda, baking powder, and salt into a bowl and set aside.

Place the oats in a glass measuring cup, pour the boiling water over top, and set aside to cool for 10 minutes.

Place the butter and sugar in the bowl of the stand mixer. Fit your mixer with the paddle attachment and beat on high speed until light and fluffy. Add the eggs one at a time, followed by the vanilla. Add the dry ingredients, followed by the oats. Mix on low speed until just combined and transfer the batter to the Bundt pan.

Bake until a knife inserted into the cake comes out clean, about 30 minutes.

Allow the cake to stand in the pan for a few minutes before turning it out onto a cooling rack to cool completely.

>>

GANACHE GLAZE

Prepare the ganache glaze, following the instructions on page 205.

Place the cooling rack with the Bundt cake on it over a cookie sheet. Pour the glaze over the cake, allowing any extra glaze to drip onto the sheet below. Place the cake in the refrigerator to allow the glaze to set completely, about 30 minutes. Use an offset spatula to transfer it to a cake plate.

Brown Butter Rice Krispie Cake

YIELD: 6 servings

INGREDIENTS

3 Tbsp (42 g) unsalted butter
5 cups (250 g) mini marshmallows
5½ cups (185 g) Rice Krispies (or your preferred brand of crispy rice cereal)
¼ cup (45 g) rainbow sprinkles, plus more for decorating
1 tsp vanilla extract

NOTE: You may be surprised to learn that Rice Krispies are not gluten-free. If you require a GF version of this recipe, be sure to check the label on the cereal box.

Growing up, my younger sister and I spent our summers with our grandmother Esther in Lime Springs, Iowa (population 471). Lime Springs had a loud siren that would sound every weekday at noon and 6:00 PM, alerting us that it was time to stop whatever we were doing and run back to our grandmother's house for lunch or dinner. Esther always had a pot of coffee brewing in her tiny kitchen, a refrigerator covered in colourful magnets, and a simple approach to food and cooking that has always inspired me. The first time I ever made Rice Krispie treats was with her. I recall standing over the big pot stirring the cereal into the melted marshmallows, her hand guiding mine. These simple treats will forever remind me of my childhood summers spent in Iowa.

METHOD

Spray a 6-inch springform cake pan thoroughly with pan spray.

Place the butter in a large heavy-bottomed saucepan over medium heat. Once the butter has melted, stir it with a silicone spatula until it begins to brown, 4–8 minutes. When you notice the butter begin to become fragrant and brown flecks collecting at the bottom of the pan, turn down the heat to low and stir in the marshmallows. Continue stirring until the marshmallows have melted and the mixture is smooth. Remove from the heat, add the Rice Krispies, sprinkles, and vanilla, and mix until combined.

Transfer the mixture to the prepared cake pan. Press it into the pan and add a few more sprinkles to the top.

Allow to set at room temperature for a few hours before you remove from the pan, slice, and enjoy.

Chocolate Cake with Luscious Milk Chocolate Icing

GLUTEN-FREE
YIELD: 10–12 servings

INGREDIENTS

CAKE

1 Chocolate Quinoa Cake (page 83)

MILK CHOCOLATE ICING

1 cup (170 g) milk chocolate callets or a good-quality chocolate bar, coarsely chopped
3 Tbsp (25 g) cocoa powder
3 Tbsp (45 ml) warm water
¾ cup (170 g) unsalted butter, at room temperature
¼ cup (32 g) icing sugar
¼ tsp salt
1 tsp vanilla extract

If you love baked goods, you'll be spoiled for choice in Nelson. There are bakeries everywhere, including several, like ours, that are tucked away in surprising places. La Ruelle Bakery, located in a quaint downtown alleyway, specializes in artisan sourdough breads. Luvafair Pastry, run by Mike, an inspired baker from the Slocan Valley, offers a weekly pop-up bakery selling to-die-for croissants and spanakopita. Across town on a leafy neighbourhood street that overlooks Kootenay Lake, L&C Bakery specializes in gorgeous traditional French cakes and pastries. I am proud to be a part of such a thriving and creative food community. Over the years, Epiphany has become known for our decadent treats and fancy cakes, like this chocolate cake paired with creamy milk chocolate icing. The icing on this cake is thick and luscious, making it ideal for applying in attractive swoops and swirls.

METHOD

CAKE

Make the Chocolate Quinoa Cake and allow to cool completely.

MILK CHOCOLATE ICING

Place the chocolate in a heatproof bowl over a pan of simmering water, making sure that the bottom of the bowl does not touch the water. Stir occasionally until it's melted and smooth. Remove from the heat and set aside to cool for 15–20 minutes.

Place the cocoa powder and warm water in a small bowl or measuring cup and stir with a fork to form a smooth paste.

Place the butter, icing sugar, and salt in the bowl of a stand mixer. Fit your mixer with the paddle attachment and beat on medium speed until light and fluffy. Add the cocoa powder mixture, followed by the melted chocolate (which should be cool to the touch but still pourable at this point) and the vanilla. Beat on high speed for a minute or two, scraping down the sides of the bowl with a silicone spatula as needed. The icing should be light and fluffy. If it's not, the melted chocolate was likely too warm when it was added. Don't worry. Just leave

>>

the icing in the mixer to cool for 15–20 minutes, scrape down the sides of the mixer, and then begin beating it again.

ASSEMBLY

Use an offset spatula to spread the icing all over the cooled cake. If you're not serving the cake immediately, store it in the refrigerator.

PIPHANY

Loaded Cardamom Banana Bread

YIELD: 8 servings

INGREDIENTS

- 1½ cups (210 g) all-purpose flour
- ½ tsp baking soda
- ½ tsp salt
- 2 tsp ground cardamom
- 2 medium-sized ripe bananas
- 1 cup (200 g) sugar
- ½ cup + 2 Tbsp (155 ml) vegetable oil
- 2 eggs
- 1 tsp vanilla extract
- ¼ cup (60 ml) buttermilk
- ½ cup (85 g) dark chocolate chips
- ½ cup (80 g) chopped walnuts

NOTE: When you're testing your banana loaf, be sure to test in more than one spot. Sometimes the knife will hit a pocket of banana and the loaf will appear to be undercooked when it's in fact done.

Banana bread is dear to my heart for a few reasons: It's delicious. It's among the first products I started producing and selling in Nelson. And it was my first published recipe. Our classic banana bread recipe was printed in the *Seasonings* cookbook published by the Nelson Public Library back in 2010 and it's been a local favourite ever since. I often have people approach me on the street to tell me how much they enjoy baking it. Here, I've added cardamom and chocolate chips to spice up our original recipe.

METHOD

Preheat your oven to 350°F. Prepare a 9 × 5-inch loaf pan (see page 27).

Sift the flour, baking soda, salt, and cardamom into a medium bowl and set aside.

Smash the bananas with a fork until no large lumps remain.

Place the sugar and oil and in a large bowl and whisk by hand until light and fluffy. Add the eggs one at a time, making sure each one is fully incorporated before adding the next, followed by the vanilla. Mix to combine. Fold in the mashed bananas using a silicone spatula.

Alternate adding the dry ingredients and the buttermilk, beginning and ending with the dry ingredients. Do not overmix. Use a silicone spatula to fold in the chocolate chips and the nuts.

Pour the batter into the prepared loaf pan and bake until a knife inserted in the loaf comes out clean, 60–65 minutes. Rotate the pan halfway through the baking time to ensure even baking.

Place the pan on a cooling rack. When the loaf is cool enough to handle, remove it from the pan and enjoy it while it's still warm, or leave it on the cooling rack to cool completely, wrap it in plastic wrap, and store in the refrigerator.

Lemon Almond Loaf

GLUTEN-FREE
YIELD: 8 servings

INGREDIENTS

LOAF

½ cup (85 g) light buckwheat flour
½ tsp baking soda
½ tsp baking powder
½ tsp salt
½ cup (100 g) sugar
3 eggs
½ cup (125 g) full-fat sour cream
¼ cup full-fat milk
¼ cup (60 g) unsalted butter, melted
1 tsp vanilla extract
1 tsp lemon extract
Zest of 1 organic lemon
2 cups (200 g) ground almonds

GLAZE

1 cup (130 g) icing sugar
Zest of 1 organic lemon
1 Tbsp lemon juice

NOTE: Be sure to use light buckwheat flour for this recipe. It's finer and lighter in texture than regular buckwheat flour, which has dark flecks because it is made from grinding the seed with the hull.

Sometimes I am hit with a strong hankering for a cup of tea and a big slice of lemon loaf. It's a very specific mood, and when it hits, nothing else will do. I've eaten gluten-free for most of my adult life, and my goal is for all of our GF products at the bakery to taste just as good as any product that contains gluten. Gluten-free baking has come a long way in the past decade. GF baked goods used to have a terrible reputation for being bland and dry, but these days with so many GF flours available it's much easier to achieve moist, delicious gluten-free baking. I have, however, noticed that GF chocolate treats seem to be available in abundance, while good vanilla and lemon GF treats are harder to come by. Given all of this, I developed this recipe for those days when that lemon loaf hankering of mine hits.

METHOD

LOAF

Preheat your oven to 350°F. Prepare a 9 × 5- inch loaf pan (see page 27).

Sift the flour, baking soda, baking powder, and salt into a bowl and set aside.

Place the sugar, eggs, sour cream, milk, melted butter, vanilla, lemon extract, and lemon zest in a large bowl and whisk to combine.

Use a silicone spatula to fold in the ground almonds and then the rest of the dry ingredients.

Transfer the batter to the loaf pan and bake until golden brown and a knife inserted in the centre comes out clean, about 40 minutes.

Place the pan on a cooling rack. Allow the loaf to cool completely.

GLAZE

Place the icing sugar, lemon zest, and lemon juice in a measuring cup or small bowl. Mix with a fork until a smooth glaze forms. The glaze should be pourable but not too runny. Add more icing sugar or lemon juice to adjust the consistency as needed.

>>

ASSEMBLY

Remove the loaf from the pan and place it back on the cooling rack. Set the rack over a cookie sheet or a large bowl to catch any drips and pour the glaze over the loaf. Allow the glaze to set for about 1 hour before slicing.

Chocolate Zucchini Loaf

YIELD: 16 servings

This loaf is a great way to enjoy zucchinis from your garden. I'm not a gardener myself, but I'm fortunate to have generous neighbours with bountiful gardens, and there's a point every summer when I have an abundance of zucchinis. When life gives you zucchinis, make chocolate zucchini loaf! The chocolate chips give this loaf a deep richness, and the allspice adds a subtle but delicious pop of flavour. This recipe makes two loaves. You can freeze one to enjoy later or gift it to your neighbour!

INGREDIENTS

2 cups (280 g) all-purpose flour
1 cup (135 g) cocoa powder
2 tsp baking soda
½ tsp salt
½ tsp ground allspice
¼ cup (60 ml) vegetable oil
1½ cups (300 g) brown sugar, packed
3 eggs
1 tsp vanilla extract
2 cups (250 g) grated zucchini (1 large or 2 small zucchinis)
½ cup (125 ml) buttermilk
1 cup (170 g) chocolate chips

METHOD

Preheat your oven to 350°F. Prepare two 9 × 5-inch loaf pans (see page 27).

Sift the flour, cocoa powder, baking soda, salt, and allspice into a small bowl and set aside.

Place the oil and sugar in the bowl of your stand mixer. Fit the mixer with the paddle attachment and mix to combine. Add the eggs one at a time, followed by the vanilla and then the grated zucchini.

With the mixer on low, alternate adding the flour mixture and the buttermilk, beginning and ending with the flour. Do not overmix. Mix only until combined and no streaks remain. Fold in the chocolate chips using a silicone spatula.

Divide the batter evenly between the two loaf pans. Place both loaves on the middle rack of the oven and bake until a knife inserted in the centre comes out clean, about 45 minutes. Be sure to test the loaves in a few spots as sometimes your knife will hit a chocolate chip and appear to be undercooked when it's in fact done. Remove from the oven and place on a cooling rack. Once cool enough to handle, remove the loaves from the pan. Slice and enjoy while warm, or cool completely, wrap in plastic wrap, and freeze to enjoy later. The loaves can be frozen for up to a month.

Jacinta Sousa

FRIEND & NEIGHBOUR

The bakery is seven steep blocks above downtown Nelson in an area called Uphill. Locals are, of course, used to the trek, but unsuspecting out-of-town customers who seek us out on foot often show up looking winded and a bit stunned. From 1925 to 1949 a streetcar carried passengers up the hill from downtown via Stanley Street. The same streetcar has since been restored and now carries passengers along Nelson's waterfront through Lakeside Park.

Uphill is a patchwork of heritage homes (some, like mine, over a hundred years old), vegetable gardens, sleek new houses, and quaint laneway buildings. My favourite part of the neighbourhood is the back alleyways. I enjoy zigzagging through them with my dogs and admiring people's back gardens.

One of my favourite back gardens is across the street from the bakery at my neighbour Jacinta Sousa's house. Jacinta travelled to Canada from her home in the Algarve in Portugal in 1959 to join her husband, Tony, who had arrived two years earlier to work for Canadian Pacific Rail. Jacinta, who spoke no English at the time, flew into Montreal and then took a multi-day train journey to Nelson. Unable to communicate, she recalls being too nervous to venture to the food car and barely eating anything on the long trip.

Jacinta and Tony eventually settled in their white stucco house in 1970. From the front, the house is modest and unassuming, but around back is where the magic happens. This is where the couple spent their springs and summers tending to immaculate rows of potatoes, beans, peppers, tomatoes, and zucchinis that cover every square inch of their back yard. Around the side of the house, there are plum and pear trees, and grapes for winemaking growing along the fence line.

When I moved into the neighbourhood in 2005, Jacinta welcomed me with fruits and veggies from her garden. She once brought me a whole plum tree in a bucket, wondering if I might like to plant it in my yard. I started baking chocolate zucchini loaf out of sheer necessity to use up all the zucchini that Jacinta was giving me.

Jacinta is now 92 years old. Tony died in 2019, but she continues to maintain her garden with some help from her son and her neighbourhood friends.

Fancy Cakes

117 An Introduction to Cake Decorating

129 Salted Caramel Cake

131 Coconut Cream Layer Cake

133 Chocolate Halva Cake

135 Lemon Buttercream Cake with Candied Lemons

139 Chocolate Mousse Cake

141 Classic Carrot Layer Cake with Candied Walnuts

145 Gluten-Free Carrot Cake

147 Espresso Cheesecake

149 Eton Mess Cake

151 Vanilla Birthday Cake with Meringues

154 *Ysauld de Montigny, Epiphany Cakes Production Manager*

AN INTRODUCTION TO CAKE DECORATING

The secret to creating a successful layer cake is having the right equipment.

If you are interested in exploring the world of layer cakes (that is, if you plan to make more than a few layer cakes a year), I suggest you invest in a few key items. It is certainly possible to make a layer cake without these things, but they make the process much simpler and a lot more enjoyable.

CAKE TURNTABLE

A turntable makes decorating cakes much easier because it rotates the cake for you as you apply the icing. I find trying to decorate a cake without a turntable incredibly frustrating. Inexpensive turntables are easy to find. But if you're serious about cake decorating, it's worth investing in a quality one.

CAKE PANS

Baking a layer cake requires multiple cake pans of the same size. You'll need the same number of pans as there are layers in the cake (a two-layer cake requires two pans, a three-layer cake requires three pans, etc). The recipes in this book are for two- and three-layer cakes. You'll require multiple 6-inch or 8-inch cake pans depending which recipe you are making. A 6-inch layer cake yields 6–10 servings, and an 8-inch cake is 10–12 servings.

Pan sizes and the number required are listed in the method of each recipe.

PIPING TIPS

I suggest investing in three or four piping tips to start. Tips with a wider opening are more versatile, so tend to be more useful. Tips with small openings are generally used for detail work and fine decorating. There are hundreds of tips out there, but I find myself reaching for the same few tips repeatedly. Some of my favourites include:

- **ROUND TIPS:** Ateco 806 and Ateco 808 (useful for applying icing between the layers and all over the outside of a cake).
- **STAR TIPS:** Wilton 4B, Wilton 1M, and Ateco 825 (useful for piping decorative borders on a finished cake).

PIPING BAGS

I find it useful to have one large bag and one small bag on hand when I am decorating a cake. I use the larger bag to apply icing between the layers and all over the outside of the cake. I use the smaller bag to pipe decorative borders and additional details.

AN OFFSET SPATULA

This will help you move the icing around on the cake and then lift the cake off the turntable once it's complete.

A STAINLESS STEEL CAKE SCRAPER

This is crucial for achieving clean, straight sides when you're decorating a cake.

SERRATED KNIFE

For trimming cake layers.

HOW TO DECORATE A LAYER CAKE

Make sure all of your cake layers are completely cool before you begin decorating and then proceed as follows.

1. Prepare your icing and fillings.

2. Place one cake layer on a cake turntable. If necessary, use a serrated knife to trim off the top so that the cake is level and flat. Cover the cake with a layer of icing about ½-inch thick, using an offset spatula to spread it right to the edges of the cake.

3. If you are adding a filling such as caramel, lemon curd, or compote, fit a piping bag with a large round piping tip and fill with icing. Pipe a border around the edge of the cake. (This border will function as a dam to keep the filling from leaking out). Add the filling to the centre of the cake. If you aren't adding a filling to your cake, move to the next step.

4. Add the next layer of cake and a second layer of icing (and filling if using). If your cake is three layers, place the final cake layer on top.

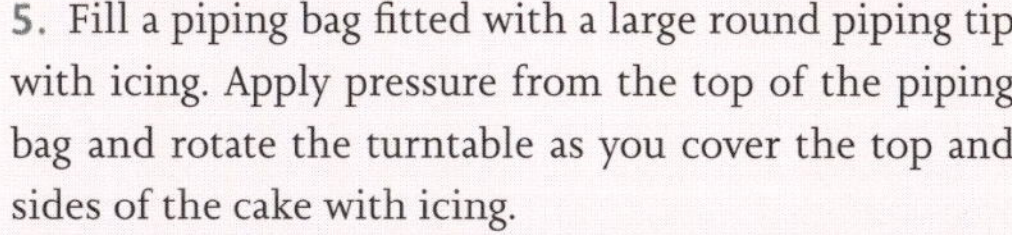

5. Fill a piping bag fitted with a large round piping tip with icing. Apply pressure from the top of the piping bag and rotate the turntable as you cover the top and sides of the cake with icing.

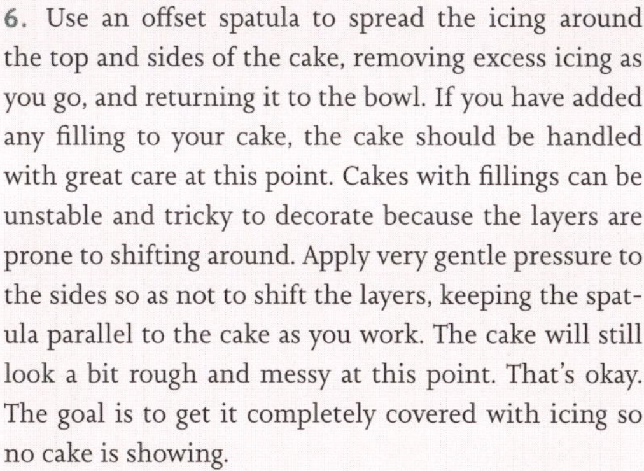

6. Use an offset spatula to spread the icing around the top and sides of the cake, removing excess icing as you go, and returning it to the bowl. If you have added any filling to your cake, the cake should be handled with great care at this point. Cakes with fillings can be unstable and tricky to decorate because the layers are prone to shifting around. Apply very gentle pressure to the sides so as not to shift the layers, keeping the spatula parallel to the cake as you work. The cake will still look a bit rough and messy at this point. That's okay. The goal is to get it completely covered with icing so no cake is showing.

7. To create smooth sides, hold a cake scraper parallel to the side of the cake, press lightly into the icing, and rotate the turntable. Place excess icing from the scraper back in the bowl. Repeat until you are happy with the sides of the cake.

8. Create a clean top edge by dragging the offset spatula from the edge of the cake inwards toward the centre of the cake, removing excess icing from the spatula as you go. Drag, remove icing, rotate turntable, drag, remove icing, rotate, and repeat until the top edge is sharp and clean.

9. Use a fresh piping bag fitted with a star tip to pipe a border around the top edge of the cake if desired.

10. Garnish the cake.

11. Chill the cake in the refrigerator on the turntable for at least 1 hour. Once the cake is completely set and chilled, use an offset spatula to transfer the cake to a cake plate.

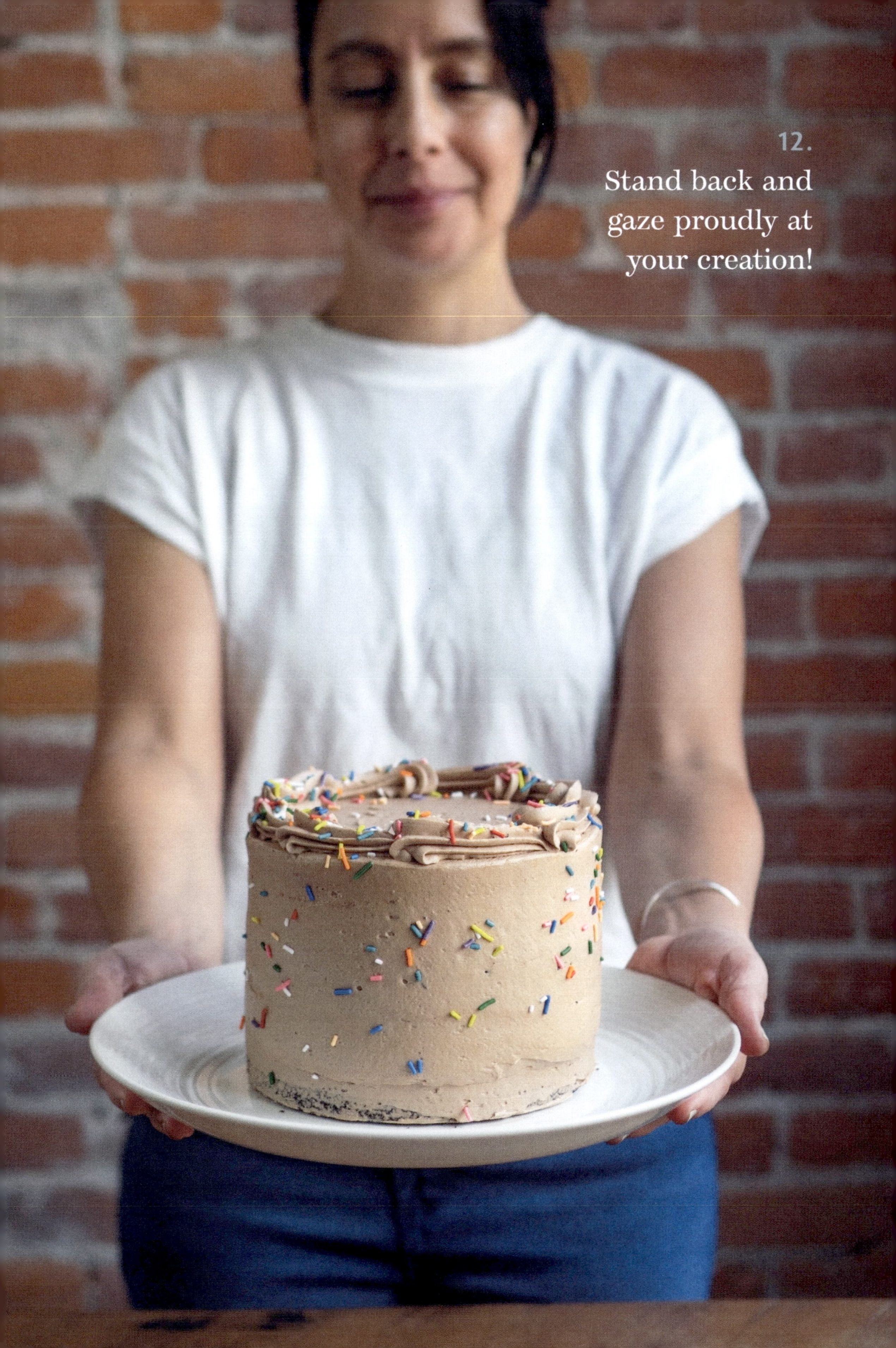

12.
Stand back and gaze proudly at your creation!

TIPS:

- Decorating cakes can feel frustrating and hard at first. Just like anything, it requires practice, so please do not be discouraged if your first attempt is not perfect. Keep in mind, if you run into trouble at any point in the decorating process, you can use the cake scraper to remove most of the icing, place it back in the bowl, and start over.
- If a cake is giving you trouble, it can be helpful to place the partially decorated cake into the refrigerator (still on the turntable) and allow the icing to chill and firm up before proceeding. Doing this will give you a much more stable cake to work with. (When you resume decorating, you may need to re-whip your icing to get it back to a nice spreadable consistency.)
- Lastly, if cake decorating feels altogether too daunting, you can adapt any layer cake recipe to make a naked cake by layering your cake, adding fillings and icings as directed, and skipping the outer layer of icing entirely. The cake will look rustic but taste just as good!

Salted Caramel Cake

YIELD: 6–10 servings

INGREDIENTS

CAKE

1 Epiphany Chocolate Cake (page 191)

GANACHE ICING

1¼ cups (300 ml) whipping cream
1 ¾ cups (300 g) dark chocolate callets

FILLING

½ batch Salted Caramel (page 210)

GARNISH

Coarse salt

People love our Salted Caramel Tarts (page 159) so much that I decided to create a cake using the same elements. Chocolate cake, ganache icing, and gooey caramel all come together to create a decadent slice of cake that tastes like a giant chocolate truffle.

METHOD

CAKE

Bake the chocolate cake layers, following the instructions for a 6-inch layer cake, and allow them to cool completely.

GANACHE ICING

Prepare the ganache icing, following the instructions on page 205.

FILLING

Prepare the salted caramel and let it cool at room temperature for at least 1 hour.

ASSEMBLY

Place one cake layer on your cake turntable, trim the top if necessary, and top with about ¼ cup (60 ml) of ganache. Using an offset spatula, spread the ganache around until you have a nice even layer about ¼-inch thick. Use a piping bag fitted with a round piping tip to pipe a border of ganache around the outer edge of the cake. Fill the centre with a few tablespoons of the caramel followed by a sprinkling of coarse salt. (Resist the urge to add too much caramel, as this will make your cake unstable and difficult to decorate.) Add the next layer of cake and top with ganache, once again spreading it out about ¼-inch thick.

Add the final layer of cake and cover the top and sides of the cake with ganache. If the cake feels unstable at any point, place it (still on the turntable) into the refrigerator to firm up for 10–15 minutes. When doing this, place a piece of plastic wrap directly onto the surface of your bowl of ganache and leave it on the counter at room temperature. This will help the ganache maintain its temperature and prevent it from cooling down too much while your cake sets in the refrigerator.

Use a piping bag to pipe a decorative border of ganache around the top edge of the cake, add the remaining caramel to the top of the cake, and garnish with a sprinkle of coarse salt.

Coconut Cream Layer Cake

YIELD: 10–12 servings

INGREDIENTS

CAKE

1 Perfect Vanilla Cake (page 193), prepared with full-fat coconut milk in place of milk

COCONUT PASTRY CREAM

1 cup (250 ml) full-fat coconut milk
¼ cup (50 g) sugar
2 egg yolks
2 Tbsp cornstarch
2 Tbsp unsalted butter, at room temperature
1 tsp vanilla extract

ICING

1 batch Vanilla Buttercream (page 199)

GARNISH

1 cup (100 g) unsweetened shredded coconut, lightly toasted

I believe that when it comes to desserts, layering textures is just as important as layering flavours. This cake combines buttery cake, silky pastry cream, crunchy toasted coconut, and smooth buttercream. The result is a cake that's chef's-kiss delicious.

METHOD

CAKE

Prepare the vanilla cake layers and allow them to cool completely.

COCONUT PASTRY CREAM

Place the coconut milk and sugar in a saucepan over medium heat, stirring occasionally. Place the egg yolks in a measuring cup and whisk with a fork. Add the cornstarch to the yolks and mix until smooth.

When the coconut milk begins to simmer, pour about half of it over the egg yolks and stir vigorously. Pour the yolk/milk mixture back into the pan, whisking constantly until it begins to thicken. As soon as you see bubbles, remove the pastry cream from the heat and stir in the butter and vanilla. Set the pastry cream aside to cool at room temperature.

ICING

Prepare the Vanilla Buttercream.

ASSEMBLY

Trim the tops of the cake layers if necessary.

Place one cake layer on your cake turntable and cover it with a layer of vanilla buttercream, about ¼-inch thick. Fit a piping bag with a round piping tip, fill it with buttercream, and pipe a border of buttercream around the outer edge of the cake. Fill the centre with cooled pastry cream. Add the second layer of cake, followed by buttercream and more pastry cream.

Add the third layer of cake and use the piping bag to distribute buttercream all over the top and sides of the cake. Use an offset spatula to spread the buttercream around and then use a cake scraper to clean up the sides of the cake. Pipe a decorative border around the top edge of the cake. Finish by gently pressing toasted coconut onto the sides of the cake with your hands.

Chocolate Halva Cake

YIELD: 6–10 servings

Halva reminds me of my childhood growing up in Bahrain. I remember streets lined with date palms and bougainvillea, and a kitchen pantry stocked with pistachios, dates, black tea, tahini, and halva. I haven't been back to Bahrain in over 20 years, but I still get homesick for those colours, that pantry, and those flavours.

INGREDIENTS

CAKE

1 Epiphany Chocolate Cake (page 191); follow instructions for a 6-inch layer cake

TAHINI ICING

¾ cup (170 g) unsalted butter, at room temperature
1 cup (130 g) icing sugar
⅓ cup (83 g) tahini
1 tsp vanilla extract

GANACHE GLAZE

½ cup (125 ml) whipping cream
¾ cup (125 g) good-quality dark chocolate callets

FILLING AND GARNISH

¼ cup (45 g) crumbled halva
¼ cup (35 g) shelled chopped pistachios

NOTES:

- Be sure to mix the jar of tahini well before adding it to the icing, as tahini tends to separate in the jar. If you use only the oily top layer, your icing will not come together properly.
- If you prefer a gluten-free cake, you can use the Chocolate Quinoa Cake (page 83) for your cake layers.

METHOD

CAKE

Bake the chocolate cake layers and allow them to cool completely.

TAHINI ICING

Place the butter in the bowl of the stand mixer and sift in the icing sugar. Fit the mixer with the paddle attachment and start mixing on low speed. Once the icing sugar has been incorporated increase the speed to medium. Scrape down the sides of the bowl as needed. Beat until light and fluffy, 3–5 minutes. Add the tahini and vanilla and mix until smooth and fully combined.

GANACHE GLAZE

Prepare the ganache glaze, following the instructions on page 205.

ASSEMBLY

Trim the tops of the cake layers if necessary.

Place one cake layer on your cake turntable, top it with some tahini icing, and use an offset spatula to spread it right to the edges of the cake. Fit a piping bag with a round tip and fill it with tahini icing. Pipe a border of icing around the outer edge of the cake and fill the centre with a few tablespoons of ganache glaze, followed by half of the halva. Add the second layer of cake followed by more tahini icing but no ganache or halva this time.

Add the third layer of cake and pipe the remaining tahini icing all over the top and sides of the cake. Use an offset spatula to spread the icing around and then use a cake scraper to clean up the sides of the cake. Pour the remaining ganache glaze on top of the cake and use the offset spatula to move it around, allowing it to drip over the sides. Garnish the cake with pistachios and the remaining halva.

Lemon Buttercream Cake with Candied Lemons

GLUTEN-FREE
YIELD: 6–10 servings

Lemon buttercream is one of our most popular cake flavours, especially for weddings. The tender lemon cake, rich creamy lemon buttercream, and tart lemon curd come together to create a dessert that's not overly sweet, and somehow delightfully rich and delicately light all at once.

INGREDIENTS

CAKE

1¼ cups (175 g) gluten-free flour blend
1½ tsp baking powder
¼ tsp salt
½ cup (113 g) unsalted butter, melted and cooled slightly
1 cup (200 g) sugar
Zest of 1 organic lemon
2 eggs
1 tsp vanilla extract
½ cup (125 ml) buttermilk

CANDIED LEMON SLICES (OPTIONAL)

1 cup (200 g) sugar
1 cup (250 ml) water
1 organic large lemon

FILLING

1 batch Lemon Curd (page 209)

LEMON BUTTERCREAM

1 batch Vanilla Buttercream (page 199)
2 Tbsp Lemon Curd
1 tsp lemon extract

METHOD

CAKE

Preheat your oven to 350°F. Prepare two 6-inch cake pans (see page 27).

Sift the flour, baking powder, and salt into a small bowl and set aside.

Place the butter in a medium bowl and add the sugar and lemon zest. Stir to combine and then mix in the eggs and vanilla.

Add half of the flour mixture to the bowl and fold to combine. Mix in the buttermilk and then fold in the rest of the flour. Divide the batter evenly between the two baking pans.

Bake until the tops are golden and a knife inserted in the centre of a cake comes out clean, 20–25 minutes.

Place the pans on a cooling rack. Once the cakes are cool enough to handle, remove them from the pans to cool completely.

CANDIED LEMON SLICES (OPTIONAL)

Line a baking sheet with parchment paper.

Combine the sugar and water in a saucepan and bring to a simmer over low heat. Thinly slice the lemon into rounds and remove any seeds. Place the lemon slices in the saucepan and simmer until the peel becomes translucent, about 20 minutes. Use a fork to remove the lemon slices from the syrup, shaking off any excess syrup, and transfer to the prepared baking sheet. Place the lemons in a single layer, being sure to avoid any overlapping.

Preheat your oven to 170°F.

>>

NOTES: The cake layers can be made a day ahead and stored tightly wrapped in the refrigerator, the lemon curd can be prepared several days ahead and stored in the refrigerator, and the candied lemons can be made in advance and stored at room temperature in an airtight container.

Bake the lemons for 30 minutes. Turn off the oven and leave them inside for an additional hour to dry out.

FILLING

Prepare the lemon curd.

LEMON BUTTERCREAM

Prepare the buttercream.

Add the lemon curd and lemon extract to the buttercream and mix to combine.

ASSEMBLY

Trim the tops of the cake layers if necessary.

Place one cake layer of on your cake turntable and cover it with a layer of buttercream, about ¼-inch thick. Fit a piping bag with a round tip and fill it with buttercream. Pipe a border of buttercream icing around the outer edge of the cake. Fill the centre with lemon curd. Add the second layer of cake.

Pipe the remaining buttercream all over the top and sides of the cake. Use an offset spatula to spread the buttercream around, followed by a cake scraper to clean up the sides of the cake. Pipe a decorative border around the top edge of the cake and add more lemon curd. Finish by gently pressing the candied lemon slices onto the front of the cake.

EPIPHANY
CAKES

Chocolate Mousse Cake

YIELD: 6–8 servings

INGREDIENTS

CHOCOLATE CAKE LAYER

¾ cup (105 g) all-purpose flour
½ cup + 1 Tbsp (112 g) cane sugar
¼ cup + 1 Tbsp (42 g) cocoa powder
½ tsp baking soda
½ tsp baking powder
½ tsp salt
1 egg
⅓ cup (80 ml) milk
⅓ cup (80 ml) warm water
2 Tbsp + 1 tsp vegetable oil
1 tsp vanilla extract

CHOCOLATE MOUSSE LAYER

1 cup (170 g) dark chocolate callets
1¼ cups (300 ml) whipping cream, at room temperature
1 tsp vanilla extract

GANACHE GLAZE

½ cup (125 ml) whipping cream
¾ cup (125 g) dark chocolate callets

There are a lot of ways to make chocolate mousse. Some methods use gelatin, egg yolks, or egg whites. At Epiphany, we use three simple ingredients in our mousse: dark chocolate, heavy cream, and vanilla. I learned how to make mousse this way when I was in pastry school at the Pacific Institute of Culinary Arts in Vancouver. This recipe requires the mousse to set for several hours (ideally overnight) before glazing, so plan to make this cake the day before you're going to serve it.

METHOD

CHOCOLATE CAKE LAYER

Preheat your oven to 350°F. Prepare a 6-inch cake pan (see page 27).

Sift the flour, sugar, cocoa powder, baking soda, baking powder, and salt into a medium bowl. Place the egg, milk, water, oil, and vanilla in a separate medium bowl and whisk to combine. Pour the liquid ingredients over the dry ingredients and whisk until smooth.

Transfer the batter to the prepared cake pan and bake until a knife inserted in the centre of the cake comes out clean, 30–35 minutes.

Place the cake pan on a cooling rack. Once the cake is cool enough to handle, remove it from the pan to cool completely on the rack.

CHOCOLATE MOUSSE LAYER

Line the inside of a 6-inch bowl (see notes) with plastic wrap, draping the excess plastic wrap over the sides of the bowl.

Place the chocolate in a heatproof bowl set over a saucepan of simmering water, making sure that the bottom of the bowl is not touching the water. Stir the chocolate occasionally until it's completely melted.

While the chocolate is melting, place the cream and the vanilla in the bowl of your stand mixer. Fit the mixer with the whisk attachment and whisk on medium speed until slightly thickened, about 4 minutes. We aren't looking for any peaks here.

>>

NOTES:

- To achieve a dome-shaped mousse cake, you'll require a bowl that's 6 inches across (you want the 6-inch cake layer to fit perfectly on top of it). The bowl can be stainless steel or glass; it doesn't matter.
- The chocolate cake layer can be made a day or two in advance and stored, wrapped in plastic wrap, in the refrigerator until you're ready to use it.

(In pastry school my instructor would say to whip the cream "slobbery," meaning whip it until it's the consistency of dog slobber. This description, while quite off-putting, is extremely helpful and I have yet to find a better way to describe the proper consistency!)

Once the cream is "slobbery," remove the bowl from the mixer. Take the bowl of chocolate off the pan of water, being sure to dry the bottom of the bowl so no water drips into your mousse.

Slowly pour the warm, melted chocolate into the cream. Gently whisk the cream by hand as you pour in the chocolate. When all the chocolate has been added, use a silicone spatula to gently fold the mousse until no streaks remain. "Gentle" is the operative word. Do not overmix or it will affect the texture, creating a dry mousse.

Pour the chocolate mousse into the prepared bowl, removing any excess so that it's level with the rim of the bowl.

Use a serrated knife to trim the cooled chocolate cake to 1½ inches tall. Place the cake on top of the mousse and gently tap the bowl on the counter to remove any air pockets Refrigerate for at least 3 hours, or up to overnight.

GANACHE GLAZE

Prepare the ganache glaze, following the instructions on page 205.

ASSEMBLY

Place a cooling rack over a cookie sheet or bowl.

Remove the cake from the bowl (the mousse and the cake layer should now be well-stuck together) and discard the plastic wrap. Flip the cake over so that the cake layer is on the bottom and the mousse is on top. Place the cake on the cooling rack. Pour the ganache glaze over the cake, allowing any excess to fall onto the cookie sheet or bowl below. Use an offset spatula to transfer the cake to a serving plate. Refrigerate until you are ready to enjoy.

Classic Carrot Layer Cake with Candied Walnuts

YIELD: 10–12 servings

INGREDIENTS

CAKE

1½ cups (210 g) all-purpose flour
1 tsp baking powder
½ tsp baking soda
½ tsp salt
1½ tsp ground ginger
1 tsp ground cinnamon
¾ cup (175 ml) vegetable oil
1 cup (200 g) sugar
2 eggs
2 tsp vanilla extract
2 cups (200 g) grated organic carrots (2–3 medium carrots)
⅓ cup (80 ml) full-fat buttermilk

ICING

1 batch Cream Cheese Icing (page 204)

GARNISH (OPTIONAL)

1 batch Candied Walnuts (page 215)

There's something incredibly humble about carrot cake. The combination of carrots, warming spices, and silky cream cheese icing makes for a cake that's both wholesome and satisfying. Customers go wild for this carrot cake. We use over 1,000 pounds of carrots a year to produce the slices we sell from our Cake Window and at the Kootenay Co-op and other retailers in the area!

METHOD

CAKE

Preheat your oven to 350°F. Prepare two 8-inch cake pans (page 27).

Sift the flour, baking powder, baking soda, salt, and spices into a medium bowl and set aside.

Place the oil and sugar in another medium bowl and whisk to combine. Add the eggs and the vanilla, mix until incorporated, and then use a silicone spatula to fold in the grated carrots.

Add half of the dry ingredients and fold until there's almost no flour visible. Fold in the buttermilk, followed by the remaining dry ingredients.

Divide the batter evenly between the two cake pans. Bake until the cakes are pulling away from the edges of the pans and a knife inserted in the centre of a cake comes out clean, 25–30 minutes.

Place the pans on a cooling rack. Allow the cakes to cool completely before decorating.

ICING

Prepare the cream cheese icing.

GARNISH (OPTIONAL)

Prepare the candied walnuts.

>>

ASSEMBLY

Trim the cake layers if necessary.

Place one cake layer on your cake turntable and top with half of the icing. Use an offset spatula to spread the icing to the edges of the cake. Add the second cake layer. Top with the remaining icing. Use an offset spatula to spread the icing around and then a cake scraper to clean up the sides of the cake.

Garnish the cake with candied walnuts if using.

Gluten-Free Carrot Cake

GLUTEN-FREE
YIELD: 10–12 servings

INGREDIENTS

¾ cup (127 g) light buckwheat flour
½ cup (75 g) brown rice flour
½ cup (50g) ground almonds
1 tsp baking powder
½ tsp baking soda
1½ tsp ground ginger
½ tsp ground cinnamon
½ tsp xanthan gum
¼ tsp salt
¾ cup (180 ml) vegetable oil
1 cup (200 g) sugar
2 eggs
½ tsp vanilla extract
2½ cups (250 g) grated carrots (about 3 medium carrots)
⅓ cup (80 ml) buttermilk
1 batch Cream Cheese Icing (page 204)

NOTE: Xanthan gum mimics the effects of gluten by adding thickness, viscosity, and moisture to gluten-free baked goods. Xanthan gum also develops elasticity and helps bind baked goods made from gluten-free flours such as brown rice, almond, and buckwheat.

We offer three versions of carrot cake at the bakery: classic, gluten-free, and vegan. Kent, one of our favourite customers, stops by the Cake Window at least once a week for a slice of carrot cake. He never seems to mind which version we're serving, as long as it's slathered in cream cheese icing. Trust me when I tell you that this gluten-free carrot cake is so tasty that even folks who aren't gluten-free will love it.

METHOD

Preheat your oven to 350°F. Prepare two 8-inch cake pans (see page 27).

Sift the flours, ground almonds, baking powder, baking soda, ginger, cinnamon, xanthan gum, and salt into a bowl and set aside.

Place the oil in a large mixing bowl and whisk in the sugar, followed by the eggs and vanilla. Use a silicone spatula to fold in the grated carrots, followed by half of the dry ingredients. Fold in the buttermilk, and then the remaining dry ingredients.

Divide the batter evenly between the two pans and bake until a knife inserted in the centre of a cake comes out clean, about 25 minutes.

Place the cake pans on a cooling rack. Allow the cakes to cool completely (you can leave them in the pan or turn them out directly onto the rack once they've cooled slightly).

Meanwhile, prepare the cream cheese icing.

Trim the cake layers if necessary.

Place one cake layer on your cake turntable and top with half of the icing. Use an offset spatula to spread the icing to the edges of the cake. Add the second cake layer. Top the cake with the remaining icing and use the spatula to spread it all over the top and sides of the cake. Use a cake scraper to clean up the sides of the cake.

Espresso Cheesecake

YIELD: 6–10 servings

INGREDIENTS

12 Biscoff biscuits
2 Tbsp unsalted butter, melted
2 cups (454 g) cream cheese, at room temperature
⅓ cup (67 g) sugar
1 Tbsp brown sugar
2 eggs
1 tsp vanilla extract
⅓ cup (80 ml) sour cream
2 Tbsp instant espresso powder

NOTE: If you prefer, the Biscoff biscuits can be replaced with four graham crackers.

I find cheesecakes so satisfying; they're just a big old hunk of delicious creamy, cheesy goodness. The base of this cake is buttery with a hint of cinnamon from the Biscoff biscuits, and the filling is rich and silky-smooth with warm notes from the espresso. The result is a delicious cheesecake that's simple and elegant. If you want to take it up a notch, whip up a batch of Salted Caramel (page 210) and drizzle it all over the cake. You won't regret it.

METHOD

Preheat your oven to 350°F. Prepare a 6-inch springform pan (see page 27).

Place the Biscoff biscuits in your food processor and pulse to create fine crumbs. Transfer the crumbs to a bowl, add the melted butter, and mix to combine. Place the crumbs in the prepared baking pan and use the bottom of a glass to press them firmly into place all over the bottom of the pan. Bake until the crust is fragrant and toasted, about 10 minutes.

Place the pan on a cooling rack. Allow the crust to cool.

Reduce the oven temperature to 225°F.

Place the cream cheese and both sugars in the bowl of a stand mixer. Fit the mixer with the paddle attachment and beat on medium speed until light and creamy, 3–5 minutes. Scrape down the sides of the bowl as needed. Reduce the mixer speed to low and add the eggs one at a time, followed by the vanilla, sour cream, and espresso powder (in that order). Mix until the espresso powder is completely incorporated and then pour the batter onto the cooled crust. Bake until mostly set (the very centre may still be a bit jiggly), about 1½ hours.

Turn off the oven and prop open the door slightly (using a wooden spoon if necessary). Leave the cake in the oven for an additional hour to cool down very slowly. This prevents cracking.

Place the cooled cheesecake in the refrigerator, uncovered, to cool completely overnight.

Once cooled, transfer the cheesecake from the pan to a serving plate and enjoy.

Eton Mess Cake

YIELD: 10–12 servings

INGREDIENTS

1 Perfect Vanilla Cake (page 193)
½ batch Meringues (page 185)
⅓ cup (43 g) icing sugar
1½ cups (354 ml) whipping cream
1 tsp vanilla extract
15–20 medium strawberries

NOTE: This cake is best enjoyed the same day that it's assembled, but the cake layers and meringues can be prepared in advance. The cake layers can be baked up to two days in advance and stored, wrapped tightly in plastic wrap, in the refrigerator. The meringues can be prepared up to 1 week in advance and stored in an airtight container at room temperature.

Eton mess is a traditional English dessert made by smooshing together whipped cream, strawberries, and meringues (hence the name "mess"). I've adapted it into a cake, but I've left the sides naked to embrace the inherent messiness of the original dessert.

METHOD

Prepare the vanilla cake layers and allow them to cool completely.

Prepare the meringues and cool them completely.

Place the icing sugar, cream, and vanilla in the bowl of a stand mixer. Fit the stand mixer with the whisk attachment and whisk the cream on medium speed until stiff peaks form.

Slice the strawberries lengthwise. Fold two-thirds of them into the whipped cream. Using your hands, crush up 10–12 meringues and fold them into the cream as well.

Trim your cake layers if necessary.

Place one cake layer on your cake turntable. Place one-third of the strawberry whipped cream on the cake and use an offset spatula to spread it right to the edges of the cake. Repeat with the next two layers of cake and the rest of the whipped cream. Top the cake with the remaining meringues and strawberries, transfer to a cake plate, and store in the refrigerator until ready to serve.

Vanilla Birthday Cake with Meringues

YIELD: 10–12 servings

INGREDIENTS

1 Perfect Vanilla Cake (page 193)
½ batch Meringues (page 185)
1 batch Vanilla Buttercream (page 199)
2 Tbsp rainbow sprinkles

I love birthdays. I'm *that* person who walks around all day telling everyone, "It's my birthday!" My sister, Rania, and I have the same birthday. We were born on the same day, four years apart, which meant joint birthday parties every year. People often ask me if I found having to share my birthday upsetting as a child. Nope. Sharing a birthday with my sister actually made it feel extra special. It still does. It's our day. Bless my mom, she always made sure to make us individual cakes. I have a favourite photo from my childhood of Rania and I joyfully prancing around the living room table with our two birthday cakes proudly displayed side-by-side. (Mine was a koala cake with Smarties for the eyes.) It's heartening, how the memory of a particular cake can stay with us for a lifetime.

METHOD

Prepare the vanilla cake layers and allow them to cool completely.

Prepare the meringues and allow them to cool completely.

Prepare the vanilla buttercream.

Trim the cake layers if necessary.

Place one cake layer on your cake turntable and top it with buttercream. Use an offset spatula to spread the buttercream right to the edges of the cake. Add the second layer of cake and repeat.

Add the final cake layer. Fit a piping bag with a round tip and fill it with buttercream. Pipe buttercream all over the top and sides of the cake. Use an offset spatula to spread the icing around, followed by a cake scraper to clean up the sides of the cake.

Decorate the cake with the rainbow sprinkles. My favourite way to apply sprinkles is to quite literally throw them at the cake. It can make a bit of a mess, but it's fun and it creates a really great haphazard effect. Using your hands, pick up a pinch of sprinkles and gently toss them onto the sides of the cake.

>>

Continue like this until you've used most of the sprinkles (reserve a few for the top of the cake).

Place the meringues on top of the cake and finish with more sprinkles.

Use an offset spatula to transfer the cake to a serving plate.

EPiPHANY
EPiPHANY

Ysauld de Montigny

EPIPHANY CAKES PRODUCTION MANAGER

When I started Epiphany Cakes in 2006, I was baking alone in my basement whenever I could find a moment (usually with a baby monitor by my side while my infant son was napping upstairs). Today, Epiphany has grown to a team of four bakers and a team member who serves customers at our Cake Window.

Ysauld, one of our lead bakers, grew up across the street. I can see her parents' house when I step out the front door of the bakery. As a teen, Ysauld developed an interest in baking and very sweetly approached me to see if I needed any help. She came in a few times and helped with grating carrots and washing dishes. At the time she was a shy, nervous, very quiet young woman. She went on to complete the culinary program at Selkirk College and move to New Zealand with her partner, Patrick, where she continued to pursue her passion for baking. When Ysauld and Patrick decided to return to Canada in 2022, she contacted me to apply for a job. We interviewed via Zoom while she was still in Wellington, New Zealand. I offered her a job, and she now works with us, preparing the cookies, cakes, and tarts that we supply to the Kootenay Co-op and other retailers in the area. (She's much chattier now than she was as a teenager!)

Tarts

159 Salted Caramel Tarts

161 Chocolate Peanut Butter Tarts

163 Fresh Berry Tarts

165 Lemon Tarts

167 Rhubarb Cherry Galette with Pastry Cream

171 Strawberry Frangipane Tarts

172 *Slava Doval, Dance Fusion*

Salted Caramel Tarts

YIELD: 6 tarts

INGREDIENTS

TARTS

1 batch Chocolate Tart Dough (page 195)
1 batch Salted Caramel (page 210)
Flaked sea salt, for sprinkling

GANACHE

⅔ cup (150 ml) whipping cream
¾ cups + 2 Tbsp (150 g) dark chocolate callets

We sell these tarts at the Cake Window and at the Kootenay Co-op. Folks go crazy for the chocolate tart shell filled with gooey salted caramel, ganache, and a sprinkle of salt. This recipe takes a bit of time and effort, but if you've ever tried one, you'll know they're absolutely worth it.

METHOD

TARTS

Prepare the dough and roll and shape the tarts into the tins, following the instructions on page 195. Chill the tarts for 1 hour, or up to overnight.

Preheat your oven to 350°F. Bake the tarts until crisp, about 12–14 minutes.

Place the tarts on a cooling rack. Let them cool completely before removing them from the tins.

While the tarts are cooling, prepare the caramel.

Carefully remove the cooled tarts from the tins. Pour warm caramel into each one, dividing the caramel evenly between the six tarts. Place in the refrigerator to cool and set, 15–20 minutes.

GANACHE

Meanwhile, prepare the ganache, following the instructions on page 205.

Pour just enough warm ganache over each tart to cover the caramel. Refrigerate the tarts again until the ganache is set, 20–30 minutes. Garnish with a pinch of sea salt.

Chocolate Peanut Butter Tarts

YIELD: 6 tarts

A chocolate tart shell filled with creamy peanut butter, chocolate ganache, and crunchy peanuts. Need I say more?

INGREDIENTS

TARTS

1 batch Chocolate Tart Dough (page 195)

PEANUT BUTTER FILLING

¼ cup (56 g) unsalted butter, at room temperature
⅓ cup (43 g) icing sugar
⅔ cup (167 g) smooth peanut butter
½ tsp vanilla extract

GANACHE

⅔ cup (150 ml) whipping cream
¾ cup + 2 Tbsp (150 g) dark chocolate callets

GARNISH (OPTIONAL)

Candied Peanuts (page 217)

NOTE: This recipe only requires a handful of Candied Peanuts, so if you choose to use the garnish, you will have leftover candied nuts.

METHOD

Prepare the dough and roll and shape the tarts into the tins, following the instructions on page 195. Chill the tarts for 1 hour, or up to overnight.

Preheat your oven to 350°F. Bake the tarts until crisp, 12–14 minutes.

While the tarts are cooling, prepare the peanut butter filling.

PEANUT BUTTER FILLING

Place the butter and icing sugar in the bowl of a stand mixer. Fit the mixer with the paddle attachment and beat on medium speed until light and fluffy. Add the peanut butter and vanilla and beat to combine.

Carefully remove the tarts from the tins. Divide the peanut butter filling evenly between the six tarts. Use an offset spatula to spread it evenly into the tart shell and then place the tarts in the refrigerator to set while you prepare the ganache.

GANACHE

Prepare the ganache, following the instructions on page 205.

Pour enough warm ganache into each tart to cover the peanut butter layer. Garnish each tart with candied peanuts (if using). Refrigerate the tarts again until the ganache is set, 20–30 minutes.

Fresh Berry Tarts

YIELD: 6 tarts

INGREDIENTS

1 batch Chocolate Tart Dough (page 195)
1 batch Pastry Cream (page 207)
½ cup (85 g) dark chocolate callets
2 cups (approx. 500 g) fresh berries of your choice

I love the feeling of being rich in berries. There's a farm on the Kootenay River in Thrums, BC, just outside of Nelson toward Castlegar, where you can pick unsprayed blueberries in the summertime. When my son, Nile, was little, we used to love going there, filling up our buckets with fresh berries, and coming home and devouring them until our fingers and mouths were stained purple. These tarts are deliciously versatile. You can use whatever berries are in season; you can't go wrong (just be sure to use fresh berries, frozen won't work). Sometimes I pile them high with blueberries; other times I use a mix of raspberries, blackberries, strawberries, and blueberries.

METHOD

Prepare the dough and roll and shape the tarts into the tins, following the instructions on page 195. Chill the tarts for 1 hour, or up to overnight.

Preheat your oven to 350°F. Bake the tarts until crisp and lightly golden, 12–14 minutes.

While the tarts are cooling, prepare the pastry cream. You want to use it while it's still warm, so don't make it too far in advance.

Place the chocolate in a heatproof bowl over a pan of simmering water, making sure the bottom is not touching the water. Stir occasionally until it's melted and smooth.

Carefully remove the tarts from the tins. Use a pastry brush to coat the bottom and inner sides of each tart shell with melted chocolate. Allow the chocolate to set for a few minutes and then pour ¼ cup (60 ml) of warm pastry cream into each tart shell. While the pastry cream is still warm, top each tart with fresh berries. Refrigerate the tarts until you're ready to serve them.

These tarts are best enjoyed on the day that they are made.

Lemon Tarts

YIELD: 8 tarts

INGREDIENTS

TARTS

1 batch Vanilla Tart Dough (page 198) (see note)

LEMON CREAM

3 eggs
3 egg yolks
¾ cup (180 ml) lemon juice (3–4 lemons)
Zest of 1 organic lemon
¼ cup + 2 Tbsp (75 g) sugar
Pinch of salt
1 cup (227 g) unsalted butter, at room temperature, cubed

GARNISH (OPTIONAL)

1 good-quality bar of white chocolate to make white chocolate shavings

NOTE: The tart shells can be rolled out in advance and stored in the freezer. No need to thaw them before baking. Just place the frozen tarts on a baking tray, add a minute or two to the baking time, and bake until golden.

The bright yellow colour of these tarts is incredibly pleasing; it reminds me of a gemstone. I remember being at pastry school and being very surprised to learn that lemon tarts are yellow mostly from egg yolks, not lemon. At the bakery, we make massive batches of lemon cream to fill these tarts every week. The process involves juicing and zesting a lot of lemons by hand (when working with lemons, I recommend that you use fresh lemon juice, not the bottled stuff). The filling also contains plenty of egg yolks and lots of butter to offset the acidity of the lemon juice, resulting in a tart that's well balanced and incredibly creamy.

METHOD

TARTS

Prepare the dough and roll and shape the tarts into the tins, following the instructions on page 198. Chill the tarts for 1 hour, or up to overnight.

Preheat your oven to 350°F. Bake the tarts until they are crisp and just turning golden, 10–12 minutes.

While the tarts shells are cooling, prepare the lemon cream.

LEMON CREAM

Place the eggs, egg yolks, lemon juice, zest, sugar, and salt in a medium heatproof bowl and whisk to combine. Place the bowl over a pan of simmering water, making sure the bottom is not touching the water. Whisk occasionally until the mixture registers 180ºF on a digital thermometer and is the consistency of loose pudding, about 15 minutes.

Remove from the heat and set aside at room temperature to cool for about 10 minutes. The mixture needs to cool down just enough so that it won't completely melt the butter when it's added. Add the butter 1 tablespoon at a time, whisking well after each addition. Once all the butter has been added the lemon cream should be smooth and pourable. If it's not, place the bowl back onto the pan of simmering water for a few minutes and whisk it until it loosens back up.

>>

ASSEMBLY

Carefully remove the cooled tarts from the tins and fill each one with warm lemon cream. Refrigerate until set, about 1 hour.

GARNISH (OPTIONAL)

Make white chocolate shavings to decorate the tarts by pulling a vegetable peeler firmly along the edge of a bar of white chocolate.

Rhubarb Cherry Galette with Pastry Cream

GLUTEN-FREE
YIELD: 8 servings

INGREDIENTS

GALETTE DOUGH

1 cup (140 g) gluten-free flour blend
¼ cup (50 g) coarsely ground yellow cornmeal (polenta), plus more for rolling
½ tsp salt
1 Tbsp honey
½ cup (113 g) unsalted butter, cold, cubed
¼ cup (60 ml) cold water

FILLING

2 cups (215 g) sliced fresh rhubarb (about 3 stalks)
1 cup (125 g) pitted dark sweet cherries, fresh or frozen (see note)
¼ cup (50 g) sugar, plus more for sprinkling
1 Tbsp (15 g) corn starch
2 tsp vanilla extract

EGG WASH

1 egg lightly beaten with 1 Tbsp of water

TOPPING

1 batch Pastry Cream (page 207)

My father grew up on a dairy farm in Iowa but raised his own family on the other side of the world in Bahrain, an island in the Arabian Gulf. When I was a kid, my dad talked about rhubarb a lot, especially rhubarb pie (his favourite). At the time, rhubarb wasn't available in Bahrain, so the pie that my dad loved so much was something I didn't taste until I moved to the United States for university. After looming large in my imagination for my entire childhood, rhubarb pie did not disappoint. I instantly loved its unique tart flavour and tender texture. These days, I maintain a deep affection for rhubarb, and love to bake with it in the summertime. My favourite way to use it is as a filling for a galette. There's something about the rustic nature of a galette that I love. It feels more casual than a pie, which I associate with big holiday meals and much fanfare. No special occasion is required to bake or eat a galette. I've included cornmeal in the crust and pastry cream as a topping to make this recipe a complete homage to my dad's childhood in the Midwest.

METHOD

GALETTE DOUGH

Place the flour, cornmeal, salt, and honey in the bowl of your stand mixer. Fit the mixer with the paddle attachment, mix on low speed to combine, and then add the butter. Mix on low speed until all the ingredients are combined and the dough looks sandy. Some small pieces of butter may still be visible. With the mixer still running on low, begin adding the water in a slow stream until the dough comes together. Remove the dough from the mixer, shape it into a block, and wrap tightly with plastic wrap. Refrigerate the dough for at least 1 hour, or up to overnight, before rolling.

Preheat your oven to 375°F. Line a cookie sheet with parchment paper.

Sprinkle your work surface generously with cornmeal.

>>

NOTES:

- If you use frozen cherries, you don't need to let them thaw first.
- Be sure to use coarsely ground yellow cornmeal (polenta) for this recipe, not corn flour or any other types of cornmeal.

Remove your dough from the refrigerator. If it is very firm, you may need to work it with your hands a bit before you begin rolling. Roll the dough into a 12-inch circle. Transfer the dough onto the baking tray.

FILLING AND BAKING

Place all the filling ingredients in a large bowl and mix to combine using a silicone spatula.

Spread the filling evenly across the dough, leaving 1½ inches of the outer edge of the dough plain. Fold the edges over the filling to create the crust. Using a pastry brush, brush the crust with the egg wash and sprinkle lightly with sugar.

Bake until the crust is golden brown, and the filling is bubbling, about 35–40 minutes.

TOPPING

While the galette is baking, prepare the pastry cream. You want to use it while it's still warm, so don't make it too far in advance.

Serve the galette warm with a generous dollop of pastry cream.

Strawberry Frangipane Tarts

YIELD: 8 tarts

INGREDIENTS

TARTS

1 batch Linzer cookie dough (page 65)

FRANGIPANE

1½ cups (340 g) unsalted butter, at room temperature
1½ cups (300 g) sugar
6 eggs
2 tsp vanilla extract
1½ cups (150 g) ground almonds

FILLING

1½ cups (450 g) strawberry jam

When I asked my staff to sample these tarts, Nadine, one of our bakers, told me that she would buy my book for this recipe alone. Frangipane is an almond cream commonly used in French pastry. It's paired here with a Linzer tart dough and strawberry jam to create a delectable tart. The almonds in the frangipane, the cloves in the Linzer dough, and the subtle sweetness of the strawberry jam all complement one another beautifully. I like to pop these tarts out of the shells as soon as they are cool enough to handle and eat them while they're still warm.

METHOD

TARTS

Prepare the Linzer cookie dough. Dust the countertop with flour and roll the dough out to ¼-inch thick. Cut 6-inch circles from the dough and press them into the tart tins. Gather up the scraps and re-roll the dough until you have eight tarts. Refrigerate the tarts for at least 1 hour, or up to overnight.

Preheat your oven to 350°F.

FRANGIPANE

Place the butter and sugar in the bowl of a stand mixer. Fit the mixer with the paddle attachment and mix on medium speed until light and fluffy, about 3 minutes. Scrape down the sides of the mixer and add the eggs one at a time, followed by the vanilla and then the ground almonds. Mix to combine, scraping down the sides of the bowl again as necessary. Fit a piping bag with a round tip and fill the bag with the frangipane.

ASSEMBLY

Remove the tarts from the refrigerator and place them on a cookie sheet. Divide the strawberry jam evenly between the tarts and spread it to evenly cover the bottom of each tart. Pipe frangipane into each tart shell, covering the jam and getting right to the edges of the tart. Bake the tarts until the frangipane is set and golden, 25–30 minutes.

Allow the tarts to cool for 20 minutes before carefully removing them from the tart tins and transferring them to a cooling rack to cool completely. (If you allow them to cool completely in the shells, they become difficult to remove.)

Slava Doval

DANCE FUSION

I wrote Slava's name on a cake long before I ever met her. In the very early days of Epiphany Cakes, Slava's partner, Neil, sauntered into the bakery requesting a massive chocolate slab cake with "Happy Birthday Slava & Paloma" written on it. As I made the cake and wrote the inscription, I thought, "What cool names. I wonder who these people are!" Little did I know that Slava, Neil, and their daughter, Paloma, would eventually become dear friends.

Slava grew up on the East Shore of Kootenay Lake. She owns and operates Dance Fusion, one of Nelson's biggest dance schools, with over 250 students of all ages. Started in 2011, the original school is in the hall of an old stone church, just a block away from Epiphany Cakes in Uphill Nelson. In the early years, Slava and her family lived on the ground level of the church and the dance classes took place in the studio above. Today, some classes still take place at the church, but most have moved to a larger studio downtown. Dance Fusion students perform hip hop, acro, jazz, and contemporary dance in an annual showcase that routinely sells out at Nelson's Capitol Theatre four times over a single weekend.

adidas

Sweets & Sundries

177 Pistachio Rose Rice Pudding

179 Salted Caramel Ice-Cream Sandwiches

181 Brownie Ice-Cream Sandwiches

185 Meringues

186 *Francyne Laliberté, Francyne's Cuisine*

Pistachio Rose Rice Pudding

GLUTEN-FREE
YIELD: 6 servings

INGREDIENTS

½ cup (115 g) jasmine rice
3½ cups (875 ml) full-fat milk
¼ cup (60 ml) maple syrup
½ tsp salt
¼ tsp cardamom powder
2 tsp rose water
1 tsp vanilla extract
¼ cup (35 g) shelled pistachios, lightly toasted and chopped
1 Tbsp organic dried rose petals (optional)

NOTE: This recipe also works well using oat milk for a non-dairy rice pudding.

Rice pudding is my comfort food, especially when it's served warm. I am generally not a fan of any recipe that requires constant stirring, but I make an exception for rice pudding (and risotto!). The rose petal garnish is entirely optional. It doesn't add much in the way of flavour, but it looks very pretty.

METHOD

Rinse the rice and place it in a heavy-bottomed saucepan. Add the milk, maple syrup, salt, and cardamom. Place the pan over medium heat and stir occasionally until the mixture comes to a simmer.

Continue to simmer, stirring every few minutes, until most of the milk has been absorbed and the pudding is slightly thickened, 30–35 minutes. (The pudding will continue to thicken as it cools.) Remove from the heat and stir in the rose water and vanilla.

Serve the rice pudding in individual bowls, and garnish with chopped pistachios and rose petals (if using). It's delicious warm or cold.

Salted Caramel Ice-Cream Sandwiches

YIELD: 12 ice-cream sandwiches

INGREDIENTS

- 1 batch Epiphany Chocolate Cake batter (page 191)
- 2 cups (500 ml) whipping cream
- 2 cups (500 ml) full-fat milk
- 1 (300 ml) can dulce de leche
- 1 tsp vanilla extract
- ½ tsp salt

NOTE: If you don't have an ice-cream maker, the recipe for Brownie Ice-Cream Sandwiches (page 181) uses store-bought ice cream.

Making your own ice-cream sandwiches might sound daunting, but it's not that hard, I promise!

METHOD

Place the canister for your ice-cream maker in the freezer at least 12 hours before you plan to make these so that it's completely frozen and ready for use.

Prepare two 9 × 13-inch baking pans (see page 27).

Prepare the chocolate cake batter and divide it evenly between the two pans. Bake until a knife inserted in the centre comes out clean, about 10–12 minutes.

Place the pans on a cooling rack. Allow the cakes to cool completely in the pans.

Meanwhile, place the cream, milk, dulce de leche, vanilla, and salt in a large bowl and whisk to combine. Transfer the mixture to the ice-cream maker. Turn on and allow to run until the mixture reaches the consistency of soft serve ice cream, 35–40 minutes.

Remove the cooled cakes from the pans. Wash the pans. Line one of the pans with plastic wrap, hanging the excess over the edge (this will make it easier to remove the finished product from the pan later). Place one cake layer into the pan top-side-down. Using a spatula, spread the ice cream evenly across the cake and right into the corners. Top with the second cake layer. Cover with plastic wrap and freeze overnight before removing from the pan and cutting into 12 portions. Store the ice-cream sandwiches in an airtight container in the freezer.

Brownie Ice-Cream Sandwiches

GLUTEN-FREE
YIELD: 8 ice-cream sandwiches

INGREDIENTS

BROWNIES

½ cup (67 g) cocoa powder
¼ tsp salt
¾ cup (125 g) dark chocolate callets
½ cup (113 g) unsalted butter
1½ cups (300 g) brown sugar, packed
3 eggs
1 tsp vanilla extract

ICE CREAM LAYER

1 (450 ml) container of ice cream, any flavour

GARNISH (OPTIONAL)

½ cup (80 g) rainbow sprinkles

When I stared eating mostly gluten-free over a decade ago, the main things that I really missed were corn dogs (don't judge me!), donuts, and ice-cream sandwiches. I recipe-tested several gluten-free ice-cream sandwiches for this book using gluten-free flour, before having an aha-moment and deciding to eliminate the flour completely. The result is a fudgy flourless brownie that's tasty and easy to bite into straight out of the freezer.

METHOD

BROWNIES

Preheat your oven to 350°F. Prepare two 8 × 8-inch baking pans (see page 27).

Sift the cocoa powder and the salt into a bowl and set aside.

Place the chocolate and butter in a heatproof bowl and set it on top of a pan of simmering water, making sure the bottom doesn't touch the water, stirring occasionally, until melted. Mix in the sugar, remove from the heat, and set aside to cool for about 10 minutes. Once the mixture is cool to the touch, whisk in the eggs and vanilla, and then use a silicone spatula to fold in the cocoa powder and salt.

Divide the batter evenly between the two baking pans. Bake until the brownies are set, about 15 minutes.

Place the pans on a cooling rack. Allow the brownies to cool completely in the pans.

Remove the cooled brownies from the pans by turning each pan over onto a sheet of parchment paper. They will be fragile, so handle with care.

ICE CREAM LAYER

Wash the two baking pans. Line one of the pans with plastic wrap hanging the excess over the edge of the pan. Empty the container of ice cream into the pan and use a silicone spatula to flatten it. Place it back in the freezer, uncovered, to harden for at least 1 hour.

>>

ASSEMBLY

Line the second baking pan with plastic wrap, hanging the excess over the edge of the pan (this will make it easier to remove the ice-cream sandwiches from the pan later). Place one brownie layer into the baking pan, top-side-down. Remove the pan with the ice-cream from the freezer and use the plastic wrap to manoeuvre the ice cream out of the pan and onto the top of the brownie. Discard the plastic wrap and place the second brownie on top of the ice cream. Press the top layer firmly into place, and then put the ice-cream sandwiches into the freezer overnight.

Remove the ice-cream sandwiches from the pan and cut into eight portions.

GARNISH (OPTIONAL): Dip each sandwich into rainbow sprinkles before serving.

Store the ice-cream sandwiches in an airtight container in the freezer for up to 1 month.

Meringues

GLUTEN-FREE
YIELD: 30 meringues

INGREDIENTS

⅓ cup (90 g) egg whites (3 whites)
⅛ tsp cream of tartar
¾ cup (150 g) sugar
¼ tsp vanilla extract

NOTES:

- Cream of tartar helps to stabilize the egg whites.
- Soft peaks are when the meringue is slightly thickened, and the peaks curl downward when you lift the whisk.
- Stiff peaks are when the whites are glossy and hold their shape without collapsing at all when you lift the whisk.
- Meringues are sensitive to moisture. Do not refrigerate them.

Meringues—a combination of whipped egg whites and sugar—are a fun way to add a whimsical flourish to any dessert. I mostly use them to garnish cakes, but you can also serve them with ice cream, dip them in chocolate, add them to a holiday treat platter, or place them on a tart or cupcake for a crunchy garnish.

METHOD

Preheat your oven to 200°F. Line a 13 × 18-inch cookie sheet with parchment paper.

Place the egg whites in the clean, dry bowl of a stand mixer. Fit the mixer with the whisk attachment and beat on medium speed until frothy. Once frothy, add the cream of tartar and continue beating until soft peaks form. With the mixer still running on medium speed, add the sugar in a slow, steady stream. Turn the speed to high and continue to beat until stiff, glossy peaks form. Add the vanilla extract and mix just to combine.

Place an open-star piping tip (such as Ateco 828) into a piping bag and fill the bag with the meringue. Working quickly, pipe 1½-inch kisses onto the prepared cookie sheet, spacing them about ½ inch apart.

Bake the meringues until crisp, about 1½ hours. Turn off the oven and leave the meringues inside for an additional 30 minutes to dry. The meringues should remain bright white. If they start to turn golden, remove them from the oven immediately.

Transfer the cooled meringues to an airtight container for storage. Meringues can be stored at room temperature for several weeks.

Francyne Laliberté

FRANCYNE'S CUISINE

When I arrived in Nelson, I was fortunate to move in next door to Francyne Laliberté and her husband, Michael Chapman. Francyne is an amazing woman and an incredible cook. From 1993 to 1998 she owned The Book Garden Café—a restaurant and bookstore—in downtown Nelson on Victoria Street with two of her friends. Francyne ran The Book Garden Café's kitchen, preparing their popular scones, signature sandwiches, and homemade soups.

By the time I arrived in 2005, she had transitioned to operating a busy catering business, Francyne's Cuisine, from the commercial kitchen in her home and supplying the Kootenay Co-op with sweet treats and salads for their deli. These days Francyne, who graciously tested several recipes in this book for me, has mostly retired from catering. But she remains busy in the kitchen cooking, preserving, and canning the produce from Michael's bountiful vegetable garden. (I have been the lucky recipient of many delicious meals from that garden over the years.) She and I enjoy a tradition of neighbourhood happy hour, and often pass cookbooks and recipes back and forth.

A Few Essential Recipes

191 The Epiphany Chocolate Cake
193 The Perfect Vanilla Cake
195 Chocolate Tart Dough
198 Vanilla Tart Dough
199 Vanilla Buttercream
203 Aquafaba Vanilla Icing
204 Cream Cheese Icing
205 Ganache
207 Pastry Cream
209 Lemon Curd
210 Salted Caramel
211 Apple Butter
213 Vanilla Extract
215 Candied Walnuts
217 Candied Peanuts
219 Crispy Chickpeas
220 *Sarah Butler, Local Author*

The Epiphany Chocolate Cake

YIELD: 8 × 8-inch slab cake, 18 cupcakes, or a 6-inch layer cake

INGREDIENTS

1¼ cups (175 g) all-purpose flour
1¼ cups (250 g) sugar
½ cup + 3 Tbsp (91 g) cocoa powder
1 tsp baking soda
½ tsp baking powder
½ tsp salt
⅔ cup (160 ml) full-fat or non-dairy milk
⅔ cup (160 ml) coffee or water, at room temperature
⅓ cup (80 ml) vegetable oil
1 egg + 1 egg yolk
1 tsp vanilla extract

This is our signature chocolate cake; you'll find it used in several recipes in this book. It's rich, moist, simple to make, and incredibly versatile. You can use it to make cupcakes, a slab cake, or a layer cake. I also use it to make ice-cream sandwiches (page 179)!

METHOD

Preheat your oven to 350°F. Prepare your baking pans according to the type of cake you're making (see below).

Sift the flour, sugar, cocoa powder, baking soda, baking powder, and salt into a large bowl and set aside.

Place the milk, coffee or water, oil, egg, yolk, and vanilla in another large bowl and whisk together until smooth.

Pour the wet mixture over the dry ingredients and whisk until smooth. Finish off by folding the batter with a silicone spatula, making sure to scrape the very bottom of the bowl and checking for any dry ingredients that may have escaped the whisk.

SLAB CAKE: Prepare an 8 × 8-inch baking pan (see page 27). Pour the batter into the pan and bake until a knife inserted in the centre comes out clean, 40–45 minutes.

LAYER CAKE: Prepare three 6-inch cake pans (see page 27). Divide the batter evenly between the pans and bake until a knife inserted in the centre of each cake comes out clean, 20–24 minutes.

CUPCAKES: Line two muffin pans with 18 paper cupcake liners. Using a (¼ cup/60ml) scoop, fill each cupcake two-thirds full. Bake until a knife inserted in the cupcakes comes out clean, 16–20 minutes.

Place the pans on a wire rack. Allow the cakes or cupcakes to cool completely on a cooling rack before decorating.

The Perfect Vanilla Cake

YIELD: 10–12 servings

INGREDIENTS

- 1¼ cups (305 ml) full-fat milk, divided
- ⅓ cup (80 ml) vegetable oil
- 3 large eggs
- 1 Tbsp vanilla extract
- 1¾ cups (350 g) sugar
- 3 cups (375 g) cake flour
- 1 Tbsp baking powder
- ¼ tsp baking soda
- ½ tsp salt
- 1 cup (227 g) unsalted butter, cut into small cubes, at room temperature

In my experience, vanilla cakes can be finicky. After much testing and tasting, I have found the reverse creaming method to be my favourite. Unlike traditional creaming method recipes (which begin by creaming the butter and sugar), reverse creaming starts by creaming the dry ingredients and the butter and then adding the liquid ingredients. Preparing the cake in this way coats the flour with butter and limits the gluten development, resulting in a moist, tender crumb. (I know, it's weird, right? It flies in the face of everything I ever learned about baking, but it works like a charm!) Be sure to bring the milk, eggs, and butter to room temperature before you begin. Don't skip this step—it's important. You may end up with lumpy batter otherwise.

METHOD

Place ½ cup (125 ml) of the milk and the oil in a small bowl. Place the remaining ¾ cup (180 ml) of milk, the eggs, and vanilla in another small bowl. Set both bowls aside for about 1 hour to allow them to come to room temperature.

Once the wet ingredients are at room temperature, preheat your oven to 350°F and prepare three 8-inch cake pans (see page 27).

Place the sugar in the bowl of your stand mixer. Sift in the flour, baking powder, baking soda, and salt. Add the butter.

Fit the mixer with the paddle attachment and beat the butter and dry ingredients on low speed until the butter is broken up into pea-sized pieces. With the mixer still running on low speed, add the milk/oil mixture. Increase the speed to medium and beat for exactly 2 minutes.

Turn off the mixer and thoroughly scrape down the sides of the bowl and the paddle. Resume mixing on low speed and add the milk/egg mixture in a steady stream. Scrape down the sides of the mixer again as needed. Mix until the batter is smooth, about 1 minute.

>>

Divide the batter evenly among the three cake pans. Bake until lightly golden and pulling away from the sides of the pans, and a knife inserted in the centre of a cake comes out clean, 20–25 minutes.

Place the pans on a cooling rack. After about 10 minutes, when the cakes are cool enough to handle, remove them from the pans and place them directly on the cooling rack to cool completely before decorating.

Chocolate Tart Dough

YIELD: 6 (4¾ × ¾-inch) tarts

This tart dough creates the crispy chocolate shell that we use for our Salted Caramel Tarts (page 159). But don't stop there. The tart shells can be filled with virtually anything: whipped cream, berries, pastry cream, ganache, or chocolate mousse. The possibilities are endless!

INGREDIENTS

½ cup (113 g) unsalted butter, at room temperature
½ cup (65 g) icing sugar
1 egg, at room temperature
1 tsp vanilla extract
1 cup plus 1 Tbsp (150 g) all-purpose flour
¼ cup plus 1 Tbsp (42 g) cocoa powder
¼ tsp salt

METHOD

Place the butter in the bowl of a stand mixer. Sift the icing sugar into the bowl with the butter, fit the mixer with the paddle attachment, and beat on low speed until the sugar is combined, about 2 minutes. Turn up to medium speed and mix until light and creamy, about 3 minutes, scraping down the sides of the bowl as needed.

Add the egg and the vanilla and mix until combined.

Scrape down the sides of the mixing bowl. Sift the flour, cocoa powder, and salt into the mixer. Beat on low speed until the dry ingredients are incorporated and the dough comes together, about 1 minute.

Turn the dough out onto the countertop and, using your hands, shape it into a block. Wrap it tightly in plastic wrap and refrigerate for at least 1 hour, or up to 2 days, before rolling. At this point, the dough can also be frozen for up to 1 month. (Thaw overnight in the refrigerator before using.)

Once the dough has chilled, remove it from the refrigerator, unwrap, and working with half of the block of dough at a time, work the dough with your hands until it's malleable enough to roll. Be careful not to work it too much, as it becomes difficult to work with when it's too warm. Dust your work surface generously with cocoa powder and roll the dough out to ¼-inch thickness, rotating it as you work to ensure it doesn't stick to the counter.

Cut 6-inch circles out of the dough (I use the bottom of a 6-inch cake pan as a guide) and form them into the tart tins. Gently press the dough into the sides of the tart tin and cut any excess from the top using a sharp paring knife. Gather up the

>>

scraps and re-roll the dough as needed. Repeat with the rest of the dough.

Prick the bottom of each tart several times with a fork and refrigerate for 30–60 minutes before baking.

Preheat your oven to 350°F.

Bake the tarts until crisp, 12–14 minutes. Cool completely before removing from the tart tins and adding your filling of choice.

Vanilla Tart Dough

YIELD: 8 (4¾ × ¾-inch) tarts

INGREDIENTS

½ cup (113 g) unsalted butter, at room temperature
½ cup (100 g) sugar
Zest of 1 organic lemon
1 egg, at room temperature
1¾ cups (245 g) all-purpose flour, plus more for rolling
¼ tsp salt

We roll a lot of tarts at the bakery, and we do it all by hand. Most of us agree that the task feels quite meditative. It's very repetitive, making it easy to get into the zone and get lost in one's thoughts. We use this tart dough as the base for our popular Lemon Tarts (page 165), but just like our Chocolate Tart Dough, the tart shells can be paired with virtually any filling. Try lemon curd, whipped cream and berries, or pastry cream with fresh peaches.

METHOD

Place the butter, sugar, and lemon zest in the bowl of a stand mixer. Fit the mixer with the paddle attachment and beat on medium speed until fluffy, 3–4 minutes. Add the egg and beat until combined, scraping down the sides of the mixer as needed.

Sift the flour and salt into the mixing bowl and beat until the dough just comes together. Transfer the dough to the counter and shape it into a block with your hands. Wrap with plastic wrap and refrigerate for 40–60 minutes before rolling. At this point the dough can also be frozen for up to 1 month. (Thaw overnight in the refrigerator before using.)

Once the dough has chilled, remove from the refrigerator, unwrap, and working with half of the block of the dough at a time, work the dough with your hands until it's malleable enough to roll. Dust your work surface generously with flour and roll the dough out to ¼-inch thickness, rotating it as you work to ensure it doesn't stick to the counter.

Cut 6-inch circles out of the dough (I use the bottom of a 6-inch cake pan as a guide) and form them into the tart tins. Gently press the dough into the sides of the tart tin and use a sharp paring knife to cut any excess from the top. Gather up the scraps and re-roll the dough as needed. Repeat with the other half of the dough.

Prick the bottom of each tart several times with a fork. Refrigerate the tarts for 30–60 minutes before baking.

Preheat your oven to 350°F.

Bake the shells until lightly golden, about 12 minutes. Cool completely before removing the tarts from the pans.

Vanilla Buttercream

YIELD: Enough to decorate 1 (8-inch) layer cake or 12 cupcakes

INGREDIENTS

6 egg yolks
1 cup (200 g) sugar
½ cup (125 ml) water
2 cups (454 g) unsalted butter, at room temperature, cut into 1 Tbsp pieces
1 Tbsp vanilla extract

There are a lot of different ways to make buttercream icing. Italian and Swiss buttercream use egg whites, French buttercream uses egg yolks, and American buttercream uses no eggs at all. The buttercream that I have always used at Epiphany Cakes is a French buttercream based on a recipe from Rose Levy Beranbaum's book, *The Cake Bible*. Rose is an American baker and cookbook author. Her books are a must-read for anyone who loves to bake. My Vanilla Buttercream is based on her Classic Buttercream recipe with a few tweaks to the original method.

METHOD

Place the egg yolks in the bowl of a stand mixer. Fit your stand mixer with the whisk attachment and begin beating the yolks on medium speed. Meanwhile, place the sugar and water in a saucepan and whisk to combine. I use a 6-inch saucepan (or something similar that's not too wide); if you use a larger saucepan, the liquid will be in a very thin layer at the bottom, making it challenging to get an accurate temperature reading. Place a candy thermometer in the pan and heat the water/sugar mixture to 238°F, about 15 minutes. At this point the egg yolks should be well-beaten and pale yellow in colour. If they aren't, increase the speed on the stand mixer for a minute or two. Once the sugar syrup has reached 238°F, turn the speed of the stand mixer to low and slowly and carefully pour the syrup over the egg yolks. Once all the syrup has been added, return the mixer to medium speed and continue mixing until cool, about 15 minutes.

With the mixer still running, add the butter 1 tablespoon at a time, followed by the vanilla extract. (To determine whether the mixture is cool enough to add the butter, place your hand on the outside of the mixing bowl. If you feel any warmth, continue beating for a few more minutes. Adding the butter when the sugar mixture is too warm will result in soupy buttercream.) Beat on medium speed until the butter is completely incorporated and the buttercream is silky and smooth. Use the buttercream immediately.

>>

VARIATIONS

CHOCOLATE BUTTERCREAM: Add ¼ cup (35g) melted chocolate (dark, milk, or white) to the vanilla buttercream and mix to combine.

LEMON BUTTERCREAM: Add 1½ teaspoons lemon extract and 2 tablespoons lemon curd to the vanilla buttercream and mix to combine.

ESPRESSO BUTTERCREAM: Dilute 1 tablespoon of instant espresso powder with a small amount of warm water (just enough to make it pourable) and mix it into the vanilla buttercream.

NOTES:

— Buttercream is very temperature-sensitive and can be finicky. Be sure to use room-temperature butter.

— If your buttercream begins to curdle after you add the butter, don't panic. This can be remedied by placing the bowl of your stand mixer with the buttercream in it over a pan of simmering water for a few seconds and then beating the buttercream on high speed with the whisk attachment. You may need to repeat the heating/beating process a few times. Be careful not to leave it on the heat for too long, or you'll end up with buttercream soup.

— If you happen to own a culinary blowtorch, you can skip the double boiler method and simply heat the outside of the bowl with the blowtorch with the mixer running on medium speed. Keep heating and mixing until the buttercream reaches the desired consistency.

— Leftover buttercream can be refrigerated for up to a week or frozen for several months. Bring the chilled buttercream to room temperature and then place it in the bowl of your stand mixer over a pan of simmering water for 10 seconds at a time as described above. Beat the buttercream using the paddle attachment first and switching to the whisk attachment once there are no longer any hard lumps (using the whisk right away can damage your whisk). Whisk until the buttercream is smooth and spreadable and use immediately.

Aquafaba Vanilla Icing

VEGAN
YIELD: Enough to decorate 2 (8 × 8-inch) cakes

INGREDIENTS

- 1 (540 ml) can organic chickpeas
- 1¼ cups (250 g) sugar
- ¼ tsp cream of tartar
- 2 cups (454 g) unsalted plant-based butter, at room temperature
- 2 tsp vanilla extract

NOTE: Stiff peaks are when your meringue is thick and glossy, holds its shape, and points straight up without collapsing when the whisk is turned upside down.

Aquafaba is the liquid in a can of chickpeas. I'm not sure who discovered that the chickpea liquid can be used to create a vegan meringue, but whoever it was deserves a prize for ingenuity. This is by far the best non-dairy icing I have ever tried. It's smooth and creamy and easy to work with. It requires a lot of mixing and a bit of patience, but it's well worth it. And if you are wondering what to do with your leftover chickpeas, I recommend the Crispy Chickpeas on page 218.

METHOD

Strain the chickpeas and reserve the liquid from the can (you should end up with about 1 cup/250 ml of aquafaba). Set the chickpeas aside to use in another recipe.

Place the aquafaba and sugar in the bowl of your stand mixer. Place the bowl on a saucepan of simmering water set over medium heat and whisk by hand until the sugar granules dissolve (test by rubbing the mixture between your fingers), 8–10 minutes.

Fit the mixer with the whisk attachment, add the cream of tartar, and beat the aquafaba mixture on medium speed until you have stiff peaks. This will take quite a while, 15–18 minutes. Once the mixture has thickened a bit you can turn the mixer up to high. Beware: If you put it on high too soon, the chickpea liquid will splash all over the place and make a mess.

Once you've got stiff peaks, add the plant-based butter a few tablespoons at a time and continue mixing on high speed. At this point the icing will likely split, curdle, and look like a disastrous mess. Don't worry. Just keep mixing on high speed until the icing comes together, 15–18 minutes. Add the vanilla and use immediately.

Cream Cheese Icing

YIELD: Enough to decorate 1 (8-inch) layer cake or 16 cupcakes

INGREDIENTS

½ cup (113 g) butter, at room temperature, cubed
1 cup (130 g) icing sugar
¼ tsp salt
1½ cups (340 g) full-fat cream cheese, at room temperature, cubed
1 tsp vanilla extract

People are passionate about cream cheese icing, and I completely understand why—it's delicious! I once had a bride, who had ordered a carrot cake wedding cake, request a large mason jar full of extra icing for her cream cheese-loving groom. Cream cheese icing is commonly featured with carrot cake, but don't stop there. It's delicious paired with virtually *any* cake. Try it with the Epiphany Chocolate Cake (page 191), in place of the ganache glaze on our Quinoa Cake (page 83), or on Vanilla Funfetti Cupcakes (page 87).

METHOD

Place the butter in the bowl of a stand mixer. Sift in the icing sugar and salt. Fit the mixer with the paddle attachment and beat on medium speed until light and fluffy, about 3 minutes. Scrape down the sides of the bowl as needed. With the mixer running on low, add the cream cheese a few tablespoons at a time. Increase the speed to medium and beat until light and creamy, about 2 minutes, scraping down the sides of the bowl as needed. Add the vanilla and beat until combined. Use immediately.

Any leftover cream cheese icing can be stored in an airtight container for up to 1 week in the refrigerator. Leftover cream cheese icing will harden in the refrigerator. Use the stand mixer fitted with the paddle attachment to beat it until it's light and spreadable, 3–5 minutes.

Ganache

GLUTEN-FREE
YIELD: Enough to glaze 1 (6-inch) cake

INGREDIENTS

- ¾ cup (125 g) dark chocolate callets or a good-quality chocolate bar, coarsely chopped
- ½ cup (125 ml) whipping cream

Ganache—a combination of cream and chocolate—is one of my favourite things. It's luscious, velvety, rich, and delicious; and you will notice that it's featured in quite a few recipes in this book. Ganache is also incredibly versatile. When it's warm it can be poured onto a cake as a glaze, and when cooled down it can be used as an icing for a cake or rolled into truffles. When I was in university, I worked at a chocolate shop that added ganache to warm milk to make the most decadent hot chocolate. At Epiphany we use ganache as the glaze for our popular Epiphany Chocolate Slab Cake (page 79) and Chocolate Mousse Cake (page 139); as a filling for our Salted Caramel Tarts (page 159); and as an icing for our Salted Caramel Cake (page 129). The basic method for ganache is the same whether you use it for a glaze, a filling, or truffles, but the cooling instructions vary depending on how you plan to use it.

In this book, when a recipe calls for ganache, the required quantities of chocolate and whipping cream are specified in each recipe's ingredient list. The following is a base recipe for dark chocolate ganache followed by instructions for the various ways to use it.

METHOD

Place the chocolate in a heatproof bowl. (If you're using a chocolate bar be sure to roughly chop it into small pieces.) Bring the cream to a simmer over medium heat and pour it over the chocolate. (Do not allow the cream to boil). Allow the mixture to stand without stirring for 5 minutes and then whisk until smooth.

FOR TARTS: Pour the warm ganache immediately into your tart.

FOR A GANACHE GLAZE OR DRIP: Allow the ganache to cool at room temperature until slightly thickened and glossy, about 10 minutes, and then pour it over your cake. Slightly cooling the ganache when it is being used as a glaze will prevent it from being too thin and rolling right off of the cake. Ganache that's poured too warm won't have a smooth, shiny, luxurious finish. If this happens, don't worry. Just cool your bowl of ganache a bit more, and then pour a second layer onto the cake.

>>

NOTES:

- Always use good-quality chocolate, not chocolate chips, when making ganache.
- Ganache can be temperamental and will split if it's heated too much or mixed too much. Be gentle with it. Heat it gently; mix it gently.
- This ganache recipe can be easily adjusted by using a 1:1 ratio of cream to chocolate (for example, 100 g dark chocolate and 100 ml whipping cream). Keep in mind, the 1:1 ratio won't work if you're measuring by volume with cups. It only works when measuring your chocolate by weight and liquid ingredients by volume.
- This recipe is for dark chocolate ganache. The ratios for milk chocolate and white chocolate ganache are different. Milk chocolate ganache uses a 2:1 ratio (two parts chocolate, one part cream), White chocolate ganache is a 3:1 ratio (three parts chocolate, one part cream). I don't often work with milk or white chocolate ganache, so I won't go into more detail about them here, but if you're interested, you can find lots of recipes and information online.

FOR GANACHE ICING OR FILLING: To use ganache as a pipeable, spreadable filling for cakes or cookies, let it cool at room temperature, gently stirring occasionally, until it has thickened to the consistency of peanut butter. (The "peanut butter" consistency we are looking for is that of conventional peanut butter, not the natural stuff.) This will take anywhere from 1 to 3 hours, depending on the time of year and the temperature of your home. When the ganache reaches that perfect spreadable consistency, act quickly, because it will become difficult to work with as it cools. You have a small window of time to use the ganache when it's at the perfect spreadable consistency. If you miss the window and it cools down and stiffens too much, place the bowl of ganache over a saucepan of low-simmering water to warm it up, and then cool it down again.

FOR TRUFFLES: Pour the ganache onto a tray lined with plastic wrap and refrigerate until completely set, at least 3 hours or up to overnight. Coat your hands with cocoa powder, break off small pieces of the cold ganache, and roll it into bite-sized balls. Roll the truffles in cocoa powder and store in an airtight container in the refrigerator.

FOR COCOA: Stir 2–3 tablespoons of ganache into a cup of warm milk to create a decadent cup of hot cocoa.

STORAGE & REHEATING: Store any leftover ganache in an airtight container in the refrigerator for a week or the freezer for up to a month. Ganache can be reheated by placing it in a heatproof bowl over a pan of barely simmering water. Once it begins to melt remove from the heat and stir until smooth. Leftover ganache can be finicky and prone to splitting, so be sure not to stir it too vigorously or overheat it.

Pastry Cream

GLUTEN-FREE
YIELD: 2 cups (500 ml) pastry cream

INGREDIENTS

2 cups (500 ml) full-fat milk
½ cup (100 g) sugar
4 egg yolks
¼ cup (30 g) cornstarch
¼ cup (57 g) unsalted butter
1 tsp vanilla extract

NOTE: It's best not to reheat this pastry cream. To reuse leftover pastry cream once it's been refrigerated, use a whisk to stir vigorously and loosen it up.

Pastry cream is a delectable custard commonly used in eclairs, cream puffs, tarts, and donuts. In this book you'll find it as a topping for Rhubarb Cherry Galette (page 167) and a filling for our Fresh Berry Tarts (page 163). Pastry cream is delicious served warm or cold.

METHOD

Place the milk and sugar in a saucepan over medium heat.

Place the egg yolks in a glass measuring cup and mix with a fork. Add the cornstarch and mix until smooth.

When the milk begins to simmer, pour about half of it over the egg yolks and stir vigorously with a fork. Pour the yolk/milk mixture back into the saucepan and use a whisk to stir constantly until it begins to thicken. This generally only takes a minute or two. Once you see bubbles, remove the saucepan from the heat and stir in the butter and the vanilla.

Use the warm pastry cream immediately if you're pouring into tart shells or serving it as a topping for a galette. If you plan to use it in a cake, let it cool completely in the refrigerator before using. Place a piece of plastic wrap directly on the surface of the pastry cream (this helps to avoid a skin forming on the surface). Store leftover pastry cream in the refrigerator for 2–3 days.

Lemon Curd

YIELD: 1½ cups (375 ml) curd

INGREDIENTS

1 cup (200 g) sugar
3–4 organic large lemons
4 eggs
2 Tbsp (30 g) unsalted butter
A pinch of salt

I mostly use lemon curd as a cake filling, but there are so many other ways to enjoy it. Dollop it over yogurt or ice cream, serve it with fresh fruit and meringues, roll it into a crêpe, or spread it onto your morning pancakes. It also makes a pretty gift packaged in a mason jar with some ribbon (just be sure to keep it refrigerated).

METHOD

Place the sugar in a heatproof bowl. Zest one of the lemons into the bowl with the sugar. Be careful to remove only the yellow part of the skin, not the white part underneath, which is bitter.

Juice all the lemons. Measure ½ cup (125 ml) of lemon juice, pour it over the sugar, and whisk to combine. Add the eggs and whisk well. Add the butter and the salt (you don't need to whisk them in, just place them on top and they'll melt in). Place the bowl over a saucepan of simmering water, making sure the bottom is not touching the water. Stir frequently until the curd reaches 170°F, about 20–25 minutes. Strain the curd through a fine mesh sieve to remove any stray bits of pulp or seeds. Transfer to an airtight container and store in the refrigerator.

If you're using the curd as the filling for a cake, cool it completely before using it.

Salted Caramel

GLUTEN-FREE
YIELD: 1¼ cups (300 ml), enough to fill 6 (4¾ × ¾-inch) tarts

INGREDIENTS

⅓ cup (80 ml) water
1 cup (200 g) sugar
¼ cup (90 g) light corn syrup
½ tsp salt
⅓ cup (80 ml) whipping cream
3 Tbsp (42 g) unsalted butter, room temperature, cubed
1 tsp vanilla extract

Salted caramel is an incredibly versatile ingredient. In this book it's used as a filling for a tart, layered into a cake, and sandwiched into cookies. My son, Nile, loves caramel and Cinnamon Toast Crunch cereal. So, for his 16th birthday I made him a cinnamon cake with loads of this gooey caramel between the layers. I trust you'll also find countless ways to enjoy this delectable stuff.

METHOD

Place the water in a saucepan, followed by the sugar, corn syrup, and salt. Place the pan over medium heat and cook without stirring until the caramel begins to turn an amber colour around the edges and registers 340°F on a candy thermometer, about 15 minutes. Remove from the heat and very carefully add the cream, butter, and vanilla. (The mixture will bubble violently and possibly splatter.) Stir to combine using a silicone spatula. If the caramel is still looking light, you can put it back onto the heat for another few minutes until it's a nice, deep caramel colour.

The caramel can be used immediately if you're pouring it into tart shells. Be sure to cool it to room temperature if you're using it as a filling in a cake.

It can be refrigerated for up to 1 week. I suggest storing it in the saucepan that it was made in. Gently reheat on low heat until warm. Do not allow it to boil.

Apple Butter

YIELD: 1¼ cups (295 ml) apple butter

INGREDIENTS

4 cups (540 g) peeled, cored, and sliced apples (about 4 medium-sized apples)
½ cup (100 g) sugar
½ cup (100 g) brown sugar, packed
2 tsp ground cinnamon
¼ tsp salt
⅛ tsp ground cloves
2 tsp vanilla extract

NOTES:

— My favourite apples to use for apple butter are Ambrosia, Gala, and McIntosh.
— This recipe can be doubled if you'd like a larger quantity.

Apple butter is so simple to make. It just requires a bit of time in the crockpot. I first made apple butter after a friend won a local pie contest with her apple butter pie. Intrigued, I immediately went to the Co-op, bought a large bag of apples, and made (and devoured) my first batch. Since then, I've discovered so many ways to enjoy this delicious stuff. I have baked it into tarts, served it with pancakes, dolloped it over ice cream and oatmeal, and eventually I developed our Apple Butter Blondie recipe (page 39) for the Cake Window.

METHOD

Combine the apples with both sugars, the cinnamon, salt, and ground cloves in a large bowl and mix until the apples are well coated. Transfer the mixture to a crockpot and cook on low heat until the apples are soft and fragrant, 8 hours.

Transfer the warm apples to a blender or food processor and blend until completely smooth. Return the mixture to the crockpot, add the vanilla, and cook, uncovered, on low for 1 hour. This additional hour of cooking time creates a delicious layer of flavour by caramelizing the apple butter.

Cool the apple butter completely and then transfer to an airtight container. Apple butter can be stored in the refrigerator for up to 3 weeks or frozen for up to 12 months.

FEB 10 '23

Vanilla Extract

YIELD: 2 cups (500 ml) vanilla extract

INGREDIENTS

56 g vanilla beans (16–20 beans)
2 cups (500 ml) vodka, rum, or bourbon

Vanilla is one of my favourite smells in the entire world, along with rose geranium, freshly cut grass, sandalwood, and ponderosa pine (which, incidentally, smells like vanilla when the sun hits it). There's a particular ponderosa pine tree on the Pulpit Rock trail on the North Shore in Nelson that I love to take deep whiffs of when I hike there on warm summer days. But I digress! I started making my own vanilla extract to give as gifts during the holidays and was instantly enchanted by the process. Making the extract is simple but it requires patience, as it takes 9–12 months to reach its prime. I generally start the vanilla I'm planning to give at Christmas in February. The vanilla beans are a bit of an investment, but the lovely thing about making vanilla this way is that you can reuse the same beans a couple of times. In addition to being cheaper than store-bought vanilla extract, it's incredibly satisfying to make. I love handling the beans: they're sleek and oily, and they leave tiny specks of delicious-smelling vanilla residue on your hands.

METHOD

Using a sharp knife, make a slit in each vanilla bean to reveal the fragrant seeds inside.

Place the beans inside a clean bottle or jar and add the alcohol. Be sure the vanilla beans are covered completely in alcohol (you may need to trim some of the beans).

Seal your bottle or jar tightly and date it so you'll know when your vanilla is ready to use. Place in a cool, dark place and give it a vigorous shake every few days. If you are using a light-coloured alcohol, you'll notice the colour deepening within a few days.

The vanilla will be ready to use in six months, and be at its prime after about a year.

Once your extract is ready, transfer it to a clean bottle or jar and store in a cool, dark place. The vanilla beans can be reused a couple of times to make more extract. Just leave the vanilla beans in the same bottle or jar and add fresh alcohol to start the process over again. (Each time you start a new batch I advise adding one or two fresh vanilla beans to the bottle to boost the flavour.)

>>

NOTES:

- To make larger quantities of vanilla extract, simply use a larger container and 28 g of vanilla beans (8–10 beans) for every 1 cup (250 ml) of alcohol.
- Vodka is tasteless, so it won't give any flavour to your vanilla extract. Rum and bourbon will impart your extract with sweet and smoky notes.

If you choose not to make more extract, be sure to scrape the vanilla beans and put all of the delicious seeds into your baking. They are full of flavour.

Candied Walnuts

GLUTEN-FREE
YIELD: ½ cup (62 g) candied walnuts

INGREDIENTS

½ cup (62 g) walnut pieces
2 Tbsp sugar
A pinch of salt

We use candied walnuts to garnish our Classic Carrot Layer Cake (page 141). They add a lovely crunch that contrasts beautifully with the creaminess of the cream cheese icing.

METHOD

Line a baking tray (any size) with parchment paper.

Chop the walnut pieces into small bits (the size of walnut crumbs that you can buy in supermarkets).

Place the walnut pieces, sugar, and salt in a saucepan over medium heat. Stir constantly until the sugar begins to dissolve, about 3 minutes. Cook, stirring constantly, until there is no sugar visible and the nuts are toasted and caramelized, 3–4 minutes.

Transfer to the prepared baking tray and set aside to cool. Once the walnuts are cool store them at room temperature in an air-tight container for up to 1 month.

Candied Peanuts

YIELD: 2 cups (300 g)

INGREDIENTS

2 cups (300 g) unsalted peanuts
1 cup (200 g) sugar
⅓ cup (80 ml) water
A pinch of salt

These nuts are utterly addictive. Use them to garnish the Chocolate Peanut Butter Slab Cake (page 77), throw a handful into a batch of brownies, or take them on your next hike to enjoy as a sweet and salty snack.

METHOD

Line a 9 × 13-inch baking pan with a sheet of parchment paper.

Combine the peanuts with the sugar and water in a heavy-bottomed pan. Cook over medium heat, stirring continuously, until the water begins to be absorbed and the sugar begins to crystallize, 12–15 minutes. Keep stirring until all the liquid has been absorbed.

Remove from the heat, mix in the salt, and transfer to the prepared baking pan to cool completely. Once cool, break apart any large chunks and transfer the nuts to an airtight container for storage.

The peanuts will keep in an airtight container at room temperature for several weeks.

Crispy Chickpeas

VEGAN
YIELD: 2 cups (360 g)

INGREDIENTS

1 (540 ml) can organic chickpeas
¼ tsp salt
½ tsp garlic powder
½ tsp smoked paprika
½ tsp ground cumin
2 Tbsp olive oil

You may wonder what a recipe for savoury chickpeas is doing in a book of desserts. Fair question! Let me explain. Our dairy-free icing is made using aquafaba (the water from canned chickpeas). Since we're constantly making our Aquafaba Vanilla Icing (page 203) and the recipe uses the water but not the chickpeas, we've always got a lot of leftover chickpeas hanging around the bakery. Our solution: toss them with some oil and spices, crisp them up in the oven, and enjoy them as a salad topper or a snack. There's often a bowl of these crispy chickpeas on the counter at the bakery that we all snack on by the handful throughout the day.

METHOD

Preheat your oven to 400°F.

Toss all the ingredients together and place them on a baking sheet (there's no need to grease or line it).

Bake for 15 minutes, remove from the oven, stir them around, return to the oven, and bake until crispy, about 15 minutes. Enjoy them warm or cold.

Sarah Butler

LOCAL AUTHOR

Sarah's first novel, *The Wild Heavens*, was published in 2020. An avid hiker and birdwatcher, Sarah's work is greatly inspired by the natural beauty of the Kootenays. When she and I hike together I am forever asking her "What kind of a tree is that? What kind of a bird is that?" She always seems to know the answer.

Prior to moving to Nelson in 2003, Sarah spent three years tree-planting and five years as a tree-planting cook in northern Ontario. As a tree-planting cook, Sarah prepared massive batches of treats and hearty meals out of a yellow school bus that had been converted into a kitchen. She recalls having to peel 50 pounds of potatoes at a time. Today, she runs her own cooking business, lovingly called The Cookshack (a nod to her tree-planting days). After Epiphany Cakes has closed shop for the day, Sarah rents our kitchen to bake the muffins, scones, and cookies she supplies to cafés in the local area. Several of her products are based on recipes that she developed as a tree-planting cook. When she's not hiking, baking, or birdwatching, Sarah is working on her second novel. (She also wrote the foreword for this book.)

EPIPH
CAKES

ACKNOWLEDGEMENTS

Anne DeGrace, thank you for being so generous with your knowledge and your time and for doing the first read of these pages.

Louis Bockner, your way of viewing the world is beautiful and your images have added a touch of magic to these pages. It was such a pleasure working with you on this project.

Sarah Butler, thank you for being an incredible friend, for providing your kind words for the foreword, for congee deliveries, and all of your support and words of encouragement. It means the world to me.

Claire Philipson, thank you. Your belief in this book and your guidance and encouragement have been pivotal. I am eternally grateful.

Cath McIntosh, you have been with me since the beginning of Epiphany, creating my first logo. Thank you for working with me to create this book. Your talent and skill are awe-inspiring. Thank you for your friendship. I'm so very grateful for you!

Nancy, Ysauld, Reiko, Nadine, Chloe, Cait, Tia, and everyone else who has worked with me at the bakery over the past 18 years: Thank you for everything you've done to make this little bakery a success. Your commitment, your ideas, and inspiration are the heartbeat of Epiphany Cakes.

Francyne Laliberté, thank you not only for being the most wonderful neighbour and generous friend, but also for testing these recipes for me and providing invaluable assistance, encouragement, and feedback.

Rayya Liebich, thank you for your friendship, and for inspiring me, and so many others, to write and to create. Love you!

Gina Sanche, Slava Doval, and Alison Dolan, thank you for cheering me on. Your friendship and support mean so much to me. I am so lucky to have friends like you.

Shelley Adams, thank you so much for your kind support of this book.

Lesley Cameron, thank you for editing this book and working with me to make it better. It was such a pleasure to work with you.

Thank you to the wonderful team at TouchWood Editions for bringing this book to life.

Nile, you are my world. I love you. Thank you for giving me purpose, and providing ever-honest feedback.

Nelson, BC, this beautiful place I am so lucky to call home. Thank you to the community who welcomed me so warmly. Thank you to every one of you who has supported this small business by ordering cakes, visiting the Cake Window, or purchasing our products around town. I am so grateful.

INDEX

A

Adams, Shelley, 97
all-purpose flour
    Apple Butter Blondies, 39
    Cherry Almond Linzers, 65
    Chocolate Tart Dough, 195–197
    The Epiphany Chocolate Cake, 191
    Gingersnaps, 59
    Our Classic Brownies, 41
    Tahini Caramel Sandwich Cookies, 67–68
    Trick or Treat Brownies, 51
    Ube Cheesecake Bars, 45–46
    Vanilla Tart Dough, 198
    Vegan Brownies with Smoked Sea Salt, 37
    Vegan Carrot Cake, 89
allspice
    Chocolate Zucchini Loaf, 111
almonds
    Cherry Almond Linzers, 65
    Double Chocolate Ginger Chippers, 61
    Gluten-Free Carrot Cake, 145
    Lemon Almond Loaf, 109–110
    Simple Lemon Bars, 33
    Strawberry Frangipane Tarts, 171
apples
    Apple Butter, 211
    Apple Butter Blondies, 39
    Vegan Carrot Cake, 89
April Cakes, 6

B

bags, piping, 25
Bahrain, 4, 133
baking sheets, 21
baking tools, 21–25
Banana Bread, Loaded Cardamom, 107
bars
    Simple Lemon Bars, 33
    Ube Cheesecake Bars, 45–46
Beranbaum, Rose Levy, 199
Berry Tarts, Fresh, 163
Birthday Cake with Meringues, Vanilla, 151–152
Biscoff biscuits
    Espresso Cheesecake, 147
blenders, 25
Blondies, Apple Butter, 39
blueberries
    Chocolate Quinoa Cake, 83–85
    Fresh Berry Tarts, 163
The Book Garden Cafe, 186
bourbon
    Vanilla Extract, 213–214
breads/loaves
    Chocolate Zucchini Loaf, 111
    Lemon Almond Loaf, 109–110
    Loaded Cardamom Banana Bread, 107
brown rice flour
    Clemmy's Homemade Dog Treats, 71
    Gluten-Free Carrot Cake, 145
    Simple Lemon Bars, 33
brownies
    Breakfast Brownies, 43
    Brownie Ice-Cream Sandwiches, 181–182
    Brownies with Pistachio Cream, 35
    Our Classic Brownies, 41
    Trick or Treat Brownies, 51
    Vegan Brownies with Smoked Sea Salt, 37
brush, pastry, 25
buckwheat
    Gluten-Free Carrot Cake, 145
    Lemon Almond Loaf, 109–110
    Simple Lemon Bars, 33
bundt cake
    Chocolate Bundt Cake with Ganache Glaze, 97–98
    Lemon Poppyseed Bundt Cake with White Chocolate Glaze, 93–95
    pans, 24
Butler, Sarah, 10, 87, 220
butter. *see also* buttercream
    about, 17
    Apple Butter, 211
buttercream. *see also* glaze; icing
    Chocolate Buttercream, 201
    Classic Carrot Layer Cake with Candied Walnuts, 141–143
    Espresso Buttercream, 201

buttercream continued . . .
Lemon Buttercream, 201
Lemon Buttercream Cake with Candied Lemons, 135–136
Vanilla Birthday Cake with Meringues, 151–152
Vanilla Buttercream, 199–201
buttermilk
about, 17
Chocolate Zucchini Loaf, 111
Gluten-Free Carrot Cake, 145
Lemon Buttercream Cake with Candied Lemons, 135–136
Loaded Cardamom Banana Bread, 107

C

The Cake Bible (Levy Beranbaum), 199
cake flour
The Perfect Vanilla Cake, 193–194
Vanilla Funfetti Cupcakes with Cream Cheese Icing, 87
The Cake Window, 72
cakes. *see also* cupcakes
Brown Butter Rice Krispie Cake, 101
Cake-ettes with Whipped Cream and Berries, 81–82
Chocolate Bundt Cake with Ganache Glaze, 97–98
Chocolate Cake with Luscious Milk Chocolate Icing, 103–104
Chocolate Halva Cake, 133
Chocolate Mousse Cake, 139–140
Chocolate Peanut Butter Slab Cake, 77
Chocolate Quinoa Cake, 83–85
Classic Carrot Layer Cake with Candied Walnuts, 141–143
Coconut Cream Layer Cake, 131
decorating, 117–126
decorating layer, 121–124
The Epiphany Chocolate Cake, 191
Epiphany Chocolate Slab Cake with Ganache Glaze, 79
Eton Mess Cake, 149
Gluten-Free Carrot Cake, 145
Lemon Buttercream Cake with Candied Lemons, 135–136
Lemon Poppyseed Bundt Cake with White Chocolate Glaze, 93–95
Olive Oil Cake with Rose Syrup, Strawberries, and Mascarpone Cream, 91–92
The Perfect Vanilla Cake, 193–194
Salted Caramel Cake, 129
Vanilla Birthday Cake with Meringues, 151–152
Vegan Carrot Cake, 89
candied
Candied Peanuts, 217
Candied Walnuts, 215
Chocolate Peanut Butter Tarts, 161
Double Chocolate Ginger Chippers, 61
Lemon Buttercream Cake with Candied Lemons, 135–136
candy thermometer, 22
cane sugar
about, 17
Chocolate Mousse Cake, 139–140
caramel
Billionaire's Shortbread, 47–49
Salted Caramel, 210
Salted Caramel Cake, 129
Salted Caramel Ice-Cream Sandwiches, 179
Salted Caramel Tarts, 159
Tahini Caramel Sandwich Cookies, 67–68
cardamom
Loaded Cardamom Banana Bread, 107
Pistachio Rose Rice Pudding, 177
carrots
Classic Carrot Layer Cake with Candied Walnuts, 141–143
Gluten-Free Carrot Cake, 145
Vegan Carrot Cake, 89
Chapman, Michael, 186
cheese
Olive Oil Cake with Rose Syrup, Strawberries, and Mascarpone Cream, 91–92
Cheesecake, Espresso, 147
cherries
Rhubarb Cherry Galette with Pastry Cream, 167–169
Cherry Almond Linzers, 65
chickpeas
Aquafaba Vanilla Icing, 203
Crispy Chickpeas, 219

chocolate. *see also* cocoa powder; dark chocolate; white chocolate
about, 18–19
Backcountry Cookies, 63
Billionaire's Shortbread, 47–49
Breakfast Brownies, 43
Brownies with Pistachio Cream, 35
Chocolate Buttercream, 201
Chocolate Cake with Luscious Milk Chocolate Icing, 103–104
Chocolate Peanut Butter Slab Cake, 77
Chocolate Zucchini Loaf, 111
Double Chocolate Ginger Chippers, 61
Lemon Poppyseed Bundt Cake with White Chocolate Glaze, 93–95
Lemon Tarts, 165–166
Our Classic Brownies, 41
Salted Caramel Ice-Cream Sandwiches, 179
Trick or Treat Brownies, 51
Vegan Brownies with Smoked Sea Salt, 37
cinnamon
Apple Butter, 211
Apple Butter Blondies, 39
Backcountry Cookies, 63
Cherry Almond Linzers, 65
Classic Carrot Layer Cake with Candied Walnuts, 141–143
Gingersnaps, 59
Gluten-Free Carrot Cake, 145
Vegan Carrot Cake, 89
citrus zester, 24
clips, metal, 25
cloves
Apple Butter, 211
Cherry Almond Linzers, 65
Gingersnaps, 59
cocoa powder
about, 18
Breakfast Brownies, 43
Brownie Ice-Cream Sandwiches, 181–182
Brownies with Pistachio Cream, 35
Chocolate Bundt Cake with Ganache Glaze, 97–98
Chocolate Cake with Luscious Milk Chocolate Icing, 103–104
Chocolate Mousse Cake, 139–140
Chocolate Quinoa Cake, 83–85
Chocolate Tart Dough, 195–197
Chocolate Zucchini Loaf, 111
Double Chocolate Ginger Chippers, 61
The Epiphany Chocolate Cake, 191
Our Classic Brownies, 41
Tahini Caramel Sandwich Cookies, 67–68
Trick or Treat Brownies, 51
Vegan Brownies with Smoked Sea Salt, 37
coconut. *see also* coconut oil
Backcountry Cookies, 63
Breakfast Brownies, 43
Chocolate Quinoa Cake, 83–85
Coconut Cream Layer Cake, 131
coconut oil
about, 18
Chocolate Quinoa Cake, 83–85
Double Chocolate Ginger Chippers, 61
coffee
The Epiphany Chocolate Cake, 191
Espresso Buttercream, 201
Espresso Cheesecake, 147
condensed milk
Billionaire's Shortbread, 47–49
Ube Cheesecake Bars, 45–46
cookie sheets, 27
cookies
Backcountry Cookies, 63
Brownie Ice-Cream Sandwiches, 181–182
Cherry Almond Linzers, 65
Double Chocolate Ginger Chippers, 61
Gingersnaps, 59
Salted Caramel Ice-Cream Sandwiches, 179
Tahini Caramel Sandwich Cookies, 67–68
The Cookshack, 220
cooling racks, 22
corn syrup
Billionaire's Shortbread, 47–49
Salted Caramel, 210
Corner Café, 5
cornmeal
Rhubarb Cherry Galette with Pastry Cream, 167–169

cream
- Chocolate Bundt Cake with Ganache Glaze, 97–98
- Chocolate Halva Cake, 135
- Chocolate Mousse Cake, 139–140
- Chocolate Peanut Butter Tarts, 161
- Epiphany Chocolate Slab Cake with Ganache Glaze, 79
- Eton Mess Cake, 149
- Ganache, 205–206
- Lemon Poppyseed Bundt Cake with White Chocolate Glaze, 93–95
- Olive Oil Cake with Rose Syrup, Strawberries, and Mascarpone Cream, 91–92
- Pastry Cream, 207
- Salted Caramel, 210
- Salted Caramel Cake, 129
- Salted Caramel Tarts, 159

cream cheese
- Cream Cheese Icing, 204
- Espresso Cheesecake, 147
- Ube Cheesecake Bars, 45–46

creaming, reverse, 193
crockpots, 25
cumin
- Crispy Chickpeas, 219

cupcakes
- Cake-ettes with Whipped Cream and Berries, 81–82
- Chocolate Quinoa Cake, 83–85
- The Epiphany Chocolate Cake, 191
- Vanilla Funfetti Cupcakes with Cream Cheese Icing, 87

cups, measuring, 27

D

dairy, about, 17
dairy-free
- Aquafaba Vanilla Icing, 203
- Backcountry Cookies, 63
- Chocolate Quinoa Cake, 83–85
- Double Chocolate Ginger Chippers, 61
- Gingersnaps, 59
- Vegan Brownies with Smoked Sea Salt, 37
- Vegan Carrot Cake, 89

Dance Fusion, 172
dark chocolate. *see also* vegan dark chocolate
- about, 18–19
- Backcountry Cookies, 63
- Billionaire's Shortbread, 47–49
- Breakfast Brownies, 43
- Brownie Ice-Cream Sandwiches, 181–182
- Brownies with Pistachio Cream, 35
- Cake-ettes with Whipped Cream and Berries, 81–82
- Chocolate Bundt Cake with Ganache Glaze, 97–98
- Chocolate Halva Cake, 135
- Chocolate Mousse Cake, 139–140
- Chocolate Peanut Butter Tarts, 161
- Chocolate Quinoa Cake, 83–85
- Double Chocolate Ginger Chippers, 61
- Epiphany Chocolate Slab Cake with Ganache Glaze, 79
- Fresh Berry Tarts, 163
- Ganache, 205–206
- Loaded Cardamom Banana Bread, 107
- Salted Caramel Cake, 129
- Salted Caramel Tarts, 159
- Trick or Treat Brownies, 51
- Vegan Brownies with Smoked Sea Salt, 37

de Montigny, Ysauld, 154
decorating cakes, 117–126
digital thermometer, 22
Dog Treats, Clemmy's Homemade, 71
Donna (customer), 12
dough
- Cherry Almond Linzers, 65
- Chocolate Tart Dough, 195–197
- Vanilla Tart Dough, 198

Doval, Slava, 172
Dubai, 5
dulce de leche
- Salted Caramel Ice-Cream Sandwiches, 179

E

eggs, about, 17
Epiphany Cakes, 10, 12–13, 52–55
The Epiphany Chocolate Cake, 191
espresso
- Espresso Buttercream, 201
- Espresso Cheesecake, 147

Esther (author's grandmother), 4, 101

Eugene, Oregon, 5
Everts, Tammy, 47
extracts, about, 18

F

Fenton & Lee, 5
flax seeds
  Backcountry Cookies, 63
  Breakfast Brownies, 43
  Vegan Brownies with Smoked Sea Salt, 37
flour. *see also* all-purpose flour; brown rice flour; cake flour; spelt flour
  about, 17
food processors, 25
Francyne's Cuisine, 186
Frangipane Tarts, Strawberry, 171
fruits, about, 19

G

Galette with Pastry Cream, Rhubarb Cherry, 167–169
ganache
  Chocolate Bundt Cake with Ganache Glaze, 97–98
  Chocolate Halva Cake, 135
  Chocolate Mousse Cake, 139–140
  Chocolate Peanut Butter Tarts, 161
  Chocolate Quinoa Cake, 83–85
  Epiphany Chocolate Slab Cake with Ganache Glaze, 79
  Ganache, 205–206
  Salted Caramel Cake, 129
  Salted Caramel Tarts, 159
garlic powder
  Crispy Chickpeas, 219
ginger
  Classic Carrot Layer Cake with Candied Walnuts, 141–143
  Double Chocolate Ginger Chippers, 61
  Gingersnaps, 59
  Gluten-Free Carrot Cake, 145
  Vegan Carrot Cake, 89
glaze. *see also* icing
  Chocolate Bundt Cake with Ganache Glaze, 97–98
  Chocolate Halva Cake, 135
  Chocolate Mousse Cake, 139–140
  Chocolate Quinoa Cake, 83–85
  Epiphany Chocolate Slab Cake with Ganache Glaze, 79
  Ganache, 205–206
  Lemon Almond Loaf, 109–110
  Lemon Poppyseed Bundt Cake with White Chocolate Glaze, 93–95
  Olive Oil Cake with Rose Syrup, Strawberries, and Mascarpone Cream, 91–92
  Simple Lemon Bars, 33
gluten-free
  Billionaire's Shortbread, 47–49
  Breakfast Brownies, 43
  Brownie Ice-Cream Sandwiches, 181–182
  Brownies with Pistachio Cream, 35
  Cake-ettes with Whipped Cream and Berries, 81–82
  Candied Walnuts, 215
  Chocolate Cake with Luscious Milk Chocolate Icing, 103–104
  Chocolate Quinoa Cake, 83–85
  Double Chocolate Ginger Chippers, 61
  Ganache, 205–206
  Gluten-Free Carrot Cake, 145
  Lemon Almond Loaf, 109–110
  Lemon Buttercream Cake with Candied Lemons, 135–136
  Meringues, 185
  Pastry Cream, 207
  Pistachio Rose Rice Pudding, 177
  Rhubarb Cherry Galette with Pastry Cream, 167–169
  Salted Caramel, 210
  Simple Lemon Bars, 33
Green, Patricia, 83
Greenleese, Amber, 37

H

Halva Cake, Chocolate, 135
Hemming, Carolyn, 83
hemp hearts
  Breakfast Brownies, 43
Higgins, Patrick, 154
honey
  Rhubarb Cherry Galette with Pastry Cream, 167–169

I

ice-cream
 Brownie Ice-Cream Sandwiches, 181–182
 maker, 25
 Salted Caramel Ice-Cream Sandwiches, 179
icing. *see also* buttercream; glaze
 Aquafaba Vanilla Icing, 203
 Chocolate Buttercream, 201
 Chocolate Cake with Luscious Milk Chocolate Icing, 103–104
 Chocolate Halva Cake, 135
 Chocolate Peanut Butter Slab Cake, 77
 Classic Carrot Layer Cake with Candied Walnuts, 141–143
 Coconut Cream Layer Cake, 131
 Cream Cheese Icing, 204
 Espresso Buttercream, 201
 Lemon Buttercream, 201
 Lemon Buttercream Cake with Candied Lemons, 135–136
 Pastry Cream, 207
 Salted Caramel Cake, 129
 Vanilla Buttercream, 199–201
icing sugar
 about, 17
 Chocolate Peanut Butter Slab Cake, 77
 Tahini Caramel Sandwich Cookies, 67–68
ingredients, 16, 28
Iowa farm, 101, 167

J

Janelle (Fenton & Lee), 5

K

Kamelia (author's mother), 4
Kent (customer), 145
kitchen scale, 22
knife, serrated, 118
Kootenay Co-op, 8, 12, 154, 186

L

La Ruelle Bakery, 103
Laliberté, Francyne, 83, 186
Larry (author's father), 4
layer cakes
 Coconut Cream Layer Cake, 131
 decorating, 121–124
 The Epiphany Chocolate Cake, 191
L&C Bakery, 103
lemon extract
 Lemon Almond Loaf, 109–110
 Lemon Buttercream, 201
 Lemon Poppyseed Bundt Cake with White Chocolate Glaze, 93–95
lemons
 Lemon Almond Loaf, 109–110
 Lemon Buttercream Cake with Candied Lemons, 135–136
 Lemon Curd, 209
 Lemon Poppyseed Bundt Cake with White Chocolate Glaze, 93–95
 Lemon Tarts, 165–166
 Simple Lemon Bars, 33
 Vanilla Tart Dough, 198
Lime Springs, Iowa, 5, 101, 167
Linzers, Cherry Almond, 65
loaves. *see* breads/loaves
Luvafair Pastry, 103
Lyra Lou Cakes, 45

M

maple syrup
 Breakfast Brownies, 43
 Double Chocolate Ginger Chippers, 61
 Pistachio Rose Rice Pudding, 177
Market Fest, 87
marshmallows
 Brown Butter Rice Krispie Cake, 101
Mascarpone Cheese, Olive Oil Cake with Rose Syrup, Strawberries, and, 91–92
McMinnville, Oregon, 5
measuring cups, 27
Meinhard Fine Foods, 6
Menzies, Neil, 172
Menzies-Doval, Paloma, 172
meringues
 Eton Mess Cake, 149
 Meringues, 185
 Vanilla Birthday Cake with Meringues, 151–152
metal clips, 25
Mike (Luvafair Pastry), 103
milk. *see* buttermilk; condensed milk; soy milk
mixer, stand, 22

molasses
Backcountry Cookies, 63
Gingersnaps, 59
Moms with Dogs, 47
Moving Mosaic Samba Band, 87

N

Nadine (baker), 171
Nelson, BC, 8, 12, 112, 172
non-dairy alternatives, about, 18
nut butters, about, 18
nutmeg
Vegan Carrot Cake, 89
nuts
about, 18
Apple Butter Blondies, 39
Brownies with Pistachio Cream, 35
Candied Peanuts, 217
Candied Walnuts, 215
Cherry Almond Linzers, 65
Chocolate Halva Cake, 135
Chocolate Peanut Butter Slab Cake, 77
Chocolate Peanut Butter Tarts, 161
Classic Carrot Layer Cake with Candied Walnuts, 141–143
Clemmy's Homemade Dog Treats, 71
Double Chocolate Ginger Chippers, 61
Gluten-Free Carrot Cake, 145
Lemon Almond Loaf, 109–110
Loaded Cardamom Banana Bread, 107
Pistachio Rose Rice Pudding, 177
Simple Lemon Bars, 33
Strawberry Frangipane Tarts, 171

O

oats
Backcountry Cookies, 63
Chocolate Bundt Cake with Ganache Glaze, 97–98
Clemmy's Homemade Dog Treats, 71
Ube Cheesecake Bars, 45–46
oil, coconut. *see* coconut oil
This Old House, 52–55
Oso Negro café, 10, 12, 41, 52
oven racks, 27
Owen, Nick, 5, 10
Owen, Nile, 7, 8, 10, 163, 210

P

Pacific Institute of Culinary Arts, 6, 139
pans
bundt, 24
cake, 21, 24, 117
cookie, 27
preparing, 27
rotating, 27
paprika
Crispy Chickpeas, 219
pastry brush, 25
peanut butter
Chocolate Peanut Butter Slab Cake, 77
Chocolate Peanut Butter Tarts, 161
Clemmy's Homemade Dog Treats, 71
Peanuts, Candied, 217
Piontek, Ken and Peggy, 5
Piontek's Bakery and Café, 5
piping bags, 25, 118
piping tips, 118
pistachios
Brownies with Pistachio Cream, 35
Chocolate Halva Cake, 135
Pistachio Rose Rice Pudding, 177
plant-based butter
alternatives, 18
Aquafaba Vanilla Icing, 203
Gingersnaps, 59
Pollock, Ferguson, 52
Poppyseed Bundt Cake with White Chocolate Glaze, Lemon, 93–95
pots, 21
processor, food, 25
pudding
Lemon Curd, 209
Pistachio Rose Rice Pudding, 177
pumpkin
Backcountry Cookies, 63
Clemmy's Homemade Dog Treats, 71

Q

quinoa
about, 17
Chocolate Cake with Luscious Milk Chocolate Icing, 103–104
Chocolate Quinoa Cake, 83–85
Quinoa 365 (Green and Hemming), 83

R

racks, cooling, 22
racks, oven, 27
rainbow sprinkles
  about, 19
  Brown Butter Rice Krispie Cake, 101
  Brownie Ice-Cream Sandwiches, 181–182
  Vanilla Birthday Cake with Meringues, 151–152
  Vanilla Funfetti Cupcakes with Cream Cheese Icing, 87
raisins
  Backcountry Cookies, 63
Rania (author's sister), 151
raspberries
  Cake-ettes with Whipped Cream and Berries, 81–82
  Fresh Berry Tarts, 163
reverse creaming, 193
Rhubarb Cherry Galette with Pastry Cream, 167–169
Rice Krispie Cake, Brown Butter, 101
Rice Pudding, Pistachio Rose, 177
Rose Rice Pudding, Pistachio, 177
Rose Syrup, Strawberries, and Mascarpone Cream, Olive Oil Cake with, 91–92
rum
  Vanilla Extract, 213–214

S

salted
  about, 17
  Salted Caramel, 210
  Salted Caramel Cake, 129
  Salted Caramel Ice-Cream Sandwiches, 179
  Salted Caramel Tarts, 159
scale, kitchen, 22
scoop, culinary, 22
scraper, cake, 118
Sea Salt, Vegan Brownies with Smoked, 37
Seasonings cookbook (Nelson Public Library), 107
seeds, about, 18
Selkirk College, 154
serrated knife, 118
sheets, baking, 21
sheets, cookie, 27
Shortbread, Billionaire's, 47–49
slab cake
  Chocolate Peanut Butter Slab Cake, 77
  The Epiphany Chocolate Cake, 191
  tips, 27
Smarties
  Trick or Treat Brownies, 51
sour cream
  Espresso Cheesecake, 147
  Lemon Almond Loaf, 109–110
  Vanilla Funfetti Cupcakes with Cream Cheese Icing, 87
Sousa, Jacinta, 112
soy milk
  Backcountry Cookies, 63
  Gingersnaps, 59
spatula, offset, 118
spelt flour
  Backcountry Cookies, 63
  Clemmy's Homemade Dog Treats, 71
  Lemon Poppyseed Bundt Cake with White Chocolate Glaze, 93–95
Spratt, Cindy, 43
Sprout vegan restaurant, 37
stand mixer, 22
strawberries
  Eton Mess Cake, 149
  Fresh Berry Tarts, 163
  Olive Oil Cake with Rose Syrup, Strawberries, and Mascarpone Cream, 91–92
  Strawberry Frangipane Tarts, 171
substitutions, ingredient, 28
sugars, about, 17
sultanas
  Backcountry Cookies, 63
sunflower seeds
  Backcountry Cookies, 63
Sweet Obsession, 6–7, 77
sweeteners, about, 17

T

tahini
  Breakfast Brownies, 43
  Chocolate Halva Cake, 135
  Tahini Caramel Sandwich Cookies, 67–68
tarts
  Chocolate Peanut Butter Tarts, 161
  Chocolate Tart Dough, 195–197

Fresh Berry Tarts, 163
Lemon Tarts, 165–166
Rhubarb Cherry Galette with Pastry Cream, 167–169
Salted Caramel Tarts, 159
Strawberry Frangipane Tarts, 171
tins, 24
Vanilla Tart Dough, 198
thermometer, candy, 22
thermometer, digital, 22
tins, tart, 24
tips, baking, 27
tools, baking, 21–25
Trafalgar school kids, 51
turntables, cake, 117

U

Uphill, Nelson, 8, 12, 112, 172

V

Vancouver Art Gallery Café, 7
Vancouver, BC, 5
vanilla
about, 18
Aquafaba Vanilla Icing, 203
Vanilla Buttercream, 199–201
Vanilla Extract, 213–214
Vanilla Tart Dough, 198
vanilla cake
Coconut Cream Layer Cake, 131
The Perfect Vanilla Cake, 193–194
vegan
Backcountry Cookies, 63
Breakfast Brownies, 43
Crispy Chickpeas, 219
Double Chocolate Ginger Chippers, 61
Gingersnaps, 59
Vegan Brownies with Smoked Sea Salt, 37
Vegan Carrot Cake, 89
vegan dark chocolate
Backcountry Cookies, 63
Breakfast Brownies, 43
Double Chocolate Ginger Chippers, 61
Vegan Brownies with Smoked Sea Salt, 37
vegetable oil, about, 18
vegetables, about, 19
Vienna Café, 10
vodka
Vanilla Extract, 213–214

W

walnuts
Apple Butter Blondies, 39
Candied Walnuts, 215
Classic Carrot Layer Cake with Candied Walnuts, 141–143
Loaded Cardamom Banana Bread, 107
whipped cream
Cake-ettes with Whipped Cream and Berries, 81–82
Chocolate Bundt Cake with Ganache Glaze, 97–98
Chocolate Halva Cake, 135
Chocolate Mousse Cake, 139–140
Epiphany Chocolate Slab Cake with Ganache Glaze, 79
Eton Mess Cake, 149
Ganache, 205–206
Lemon Poppyseed Bundt Cake with White Chocolate Glaze, 93–95
Olive Oil Cake with Rose Syrup, Strawberries, and Mascarpone Cream, 91–92
Salted Caramel, 210
Salted Caramel Cake, 129
Salted Caramel Ice-Cream Sandwiches, 179
Salted Caramel Tarts, 159
white chocolate
about, 19
Lemon Poppyseed Bundt Cake with White Chocolate Glaze, 93–95
Lemon Tarts, 165–166
Whitewater Cooks (Adams), 97
The Wild Heavens (Butler), 220

X

xanthan gum
Gluten-Free Carrot Cake, 145

Y

Yiannis and Georgia (author's friends), 91

Z

zester, citrus, 24
Zucchini Loaf, Chocolate, 111

TouchWood Editions
touchwoodeditions.com

Edited by Lesley Cameron
Cover and interior design by Jazmin Welch
Cover photography by Louis Bockner
Recipe photography by Melissa Owen
Photo on page ii by Bree Prosser
All additional photography by Louis Bockner

CATALOGUING DATA AVAILABLE FROM LIBRARY AND ARCHIVES CANADA
ISBN 9781771514255 (hardcover)
ISBN 9781771514453 (electronic)

TouchWood Editions acknowledges that the land on which we live and work is within the traditional territories of the Lkwungen (Esquimalt and Songhees), Malahat, Pacheedaht, Scia'new, T'Sou-ke and W̱SÁNEĆ (Pauquachin, Tsartlip, Tsawout, Tseycum) peoples.

We acknowledge the financial support of the Government of Canada through the Canada Book Fund and of the Province of British Columbia through the Book Publishing Tax Credit.

This book was produced using FSC®-certified, acid-free papers, processed chlorine free, and printed with soya-based inks.

Printed in China

28 27 26 25 24 1 2 3 4 5